OCEAN OF LOVE, OR SEA OF TROUBLES?

OCEAN OF LOVE, OR SEA OF TROUBLES?

Can we find God in a suffering world?

Geoffrey Harris

WIPF & STOCK · Eugene, Oregon

OCEAN OF LOVE, OR SEA OF TROUBLES?
Can We Find God in a Suffering World?

Copyright © 2016 Geoffrey Harris. All rights reserved. Except for brief quotations in critical publications or reviews, no part of this book may be reproduced in any manner without prior written permission from the publisher. Write: Permissions, Wipf and Stock Publishers, 199 W. 8th Ave., Suite 3, Eugene, OR 97401.

Wipf & Stock
An Imprint of Wipf and Stock Publishers
199 W. 8th Ave., Suite 3
Eugene, OR 97401

www.wipfandstock.com

PAPERBACK ISBN: 978-1-4982-3804-5
HARDCOVER ISBN: 978-1-4982-3806-9
EBOOK ISBN: 978-1-4982-3805-2\

Manufactured in the U.S.A.   DECEMBER 15, 2016

CONTENTS

Acknowledgments and Thanks | vii

Section One—Can We Find God? | 1

    Chapter 1: Introduction | 3

    Chapter 2: Foundations | 14

Section Two—A Suffering World—Biblical Responses | 75

    Chapter 3: The Debate in the Old Testament | 77

    Chapter 4: The Suffering Servant of Isaiah | 88

    Chapter 5: The Purpose of Suffering in the New Testament | 99

Section Three—A Suffering World—Modern Responses | 115

    Chapter 6: Setting the Scene | 117

    Chapter 7: Two Writers on Suffering—C.S. Lewis and Philip Yancey | 122

    Chapter 8: Interviews with People Who Have Known Suffering | 145

    Chapter 9: Final Reflections | 162

Bibliography | 167

ACKNOWLEDGMENTS AND THANKS

First, I would like to dedicate this book to Jane, my wife and soul mate of forty-two years. While I have been working on the book, she has fielded phone calls, kept my study as a quiet sanctuary and plied me with cups of tea at regular intervals. She has been my great companion and helper through thick and thin.

This book began life as a series of three lectures on the subject of suffering. They formed the Lincoln Cathedral Lent talks, and were commissioned by Canon Dr. Mark Hocknull, an old friend and colleague of mine, who is also Chancellor of the Cathedral. I need to thank him for setting me on the path to expanding the talks and turning them into something rather different! Several people attending the lectures encouraged me to develop them into a book.

I would like to thank the staff and patients at Lindsey Lodge Hospice, Scunthorpe, Lincolnshire for giving me their time and assistance through a number of interviews.

Special thanks, however, go to the lead chaplain of the hospice, Canon Michael Boughton, who kindly set up the interviews for me and drove me to the hospice. He was most helpful and gracious.

I also need to express my gratitude to those people I interviewed, some of whom had to recount painful events and episodes in their lives, and who, in certain cases, are suffering from serious illnesses even now.

I would like to thank staff at Wipf and Stock publishing. Much of our business has been conducted over the computer network, and I am grateful especially to Matt Wimer and James Stock, who have been invariably courteous, helpful and encouraging.

Now over to you, dear reader. As Shakespeare liked to asked his audience's forbearance; so I ask you to be merciful, in words from the finale of *The Tempest*:

> 'Release me from my bands, with the help of your good hands;
> Gentle breath of yours my sails must fill, or else my project fails,
> Which was to please . . .

SECTION ONE

CAN WE FIND GOD?

CHAPTER ONE

INTRODUCTION

THERE ARE SEVERAL SONGS with the title "Ocean of Love." One, with lyrics by Robert A. Holdt, is dedicated to Meher Baba, a twentieth century Hindu spiritual master, a man who also claimed that he was an "avatar"; that is, the manifestation of a god in human form. The song compares the infinite expanse of the divine being to a great ocean. Here is an extract:

> I am the Ocean where all have begun
> I am Beloved sublime.
> I am the Ocean where all finally come
> I am the One beyond time.

Another song called "Ocean of Love" comes from a Muslim source, and is performed by Milad Raza Qadri. It extols the virtues of God and of the Prophet Muhammad (and seems rather to confuse the two):

> He is an ocean of mercy,
> He is an ocean of love
> He is the symbol of peace
> He is the dawn of light.
> Like the sun who shines on everyone,
> He is the ray of hope who is for everyone.

Christians, by way of contrast, seem uneasy about the metaphor of "an ocean" when speaking of God, probably because it could easily imply that individual Christians are mere drops in that ocean and might lose their individuality or their personal salvation in an infinite ocean of love.

However, it is not problematic for Christians to see *life* as "an ocean of love," given that the presence of God in the world, and in the midst of life, should give rise to a sense of God's love and grace. Many signs in the world—including the importance of love in human life—would also suggest the activity of God in the world. So perhaps it would be perfectly appropriate for Christians to speak of *life as a whole* as "a sea of love."

The New Testament would appear to support this view. After all, the letter of 1 John states categorically that "God is love" and goes on to say that "whoever does not love does not know God, for God is love" (1 John 4:8). This is also developed a few verses later when we read, "God is love, and whoever abides in love abides in God, and God abides in him" (1 John 4:16). The Apostle Paul also places love at the center of human life, and asserts that self-giving love (agape) comes from God. This is of course in his paeon of praise to love in 1 Corinthians 13. John's gospel teaches that God reaches out to the world in love and sent his Son into the world out of the love he had for all people: "For God so loved the world that he gave his only Son, so that everyone who believes in him may not perish, but have eternal life." Then he clarifies: "God did not send his Son into the world to condemn the world, but in order that the world might be saved through him John 3:16–17).

Nevertheless, there is a reason why Christians may be uneasy with the metaphor of God's world as "an ocean of love." The truth is that the world is God's mission field, and it is a place where God's love finds expression; *but* it is also a dark place where evil and sin abound. Thus, the gospel of John is ambivalent about the world ("kosmos" in Greek). The evangelist certainly sees it as the creation of God and the place of God's presence and activity. However, at the same time, John regards the world as the place where God's Son is rejected and refused. It is the place where the truth is not accepted. Speaking of the Word of God, Jesus Christ, John writes: "He was in the world, and the world came into being through him, yet the world did not know him" (John 1:10). Only some accepted him and to them he gave "the power to become children of God" (v. 12).

Then in chapter 17 of John's gospel, Jesus prays for his followers to be protected from the evil and unbelief of the world (17:11), and he makes it clear that "the world has hated them, because they do not belong to the world, just as I do not belong to the world." Therefore, in John's gospel—and elsewhere in the New Testament—there is an ambivalence about life in this world. It is the place where we can come to know the love of God and the joy which only Jesus can give (John 17:13); but it is also a place of danger, of opposition to God and of hatred towards Jesus' disciples. In fact, Jesus in John's gospel sees the world as the dominion of Satan, who is called "the prince of this world" (John 12:31; 14:30). The Apostle Paul similarly regards Satan as "the god of this world" (2 Cor 4:4). So we have to concede that, according to the New Testament, this world is not only the place which gives access to God's love and displays signs of God's glory; it is also a "sea of troubles." In short, life in this world is a paradox. It can be at one and the same time "an ocean of love" *and also* "a sea of troubles."

Now we come to a Christian song called "Oceans" (made famous by the Australian New Church community called Hillsong), and the lyrics seem to compare the ordinary Christian's experience to that of Peter being called by Jesus to walk upon the water of Lake Gennesaret. Peter ventures a few steps in faith, but is afraid of the wind and the waves and then starts to sink. He cries out to Jesus, "Lord save me." Then Jesus catches him and helps him to get back in the boat (Matt 14:28–33). The song "Oceans" similarly regards the Christian's journey through life as a dangerous walk upon the waves of the sea. Storms and winds threaten and the disciple must look to Jesus for safety and for salvation.

> You call me out upon the waters;
> The great unknown, where my feet may fail.
> And there I find you in the mystery,
> In oceans deep my faith will stand.
> And I will call upon your name
> And keep my eyes above the waves.
> When oceans rise my soul will rest in your embrace,
> For I am yours and you are mine.
>
> Your grace abounds in deepest waters
> Your sovereign hand will be my guide
> Where feet may fail and fear surrounds me
> You've never failed and you won't start now.
> So I will call upon your name
> And keep my eyes above the waves.
> When oceans rise my soul will rest in your embrace;
> For I am yours and you are mine.[1]

In fact this is the very experience of most people. As the French philosopher Henri Bergson once said, "Life is, on balance, good, and worth living." Yet on the other hand, most of us recognize that life is also capable of throwing

---

1. By Hillsong United (Authors Matt Crocker, Joel Houston, Salomon Ligthelm). Song released September 2013 on the album "Zion."

many problems at us: dangers, setbacks, terrible accidents, illnesses, tribulations of all kinds . . . It is indeed a "sea of troubles," which might suddenly throw up winds, crashing waves and the peril of deep waters.

To many people this aspect of life—the sea of troubles—means that they have lost their faith in God or have come to regard God as an unjust monster. There is too much undeserved suffering, there are too many arbitrary disasters, there are too many innocent people becoming victims—displaced, dispersed or with their lives disrupted or even destroyed. All this leads people in the modern world to question faith. Whereas up until the twentieth century most people regarded God as the judge of the world, with humans as the culprits, the sinners who have spoiled a good creation; now, in the twenty-first century, God is in the dock. As Philip Yancey writes,[2] "The modern world is still pictured as a courtroom scene, as described by the ancients, but not with God as judge, setting the rules and arbitrating disputes. Rather, he stands indicted, and prosecutors are stalking across the stage jabbing their fingers at him, demanding to know why He allows a miserable world to continue, and what right He has to make such grandiose claims about His Son."

If we briefly turn to Shakespeare's "Hamlet," the eponymous hero finds himself in a quandary. His father is dead and his mother has quickly remarried—to Hamlet's uncle, his father's brother. This uncle, Claudius, has now pronounced himself king. Hamlet suspects foul play—that his father has been murdered—particularly since he himself was—and still is—the true heir to the throne. Hamlet regards his mother's behavior as incestuous, and his uncle's as treacherous. What should he do? Is it his duty to avenge his father's death, or should he remain silent and passive and allow these wrongs to go unpunished, for the sake of peace and family unity? All this leads Hamlet to see life as "a sea of troubles":

> To be or not to be; that is the question:
> Whether 'tis nobler in the mind
> to suffer the slings and arrows of outrageous fortune,
> or to take arms against a sea of troubles,
> and by opposing, end them. . . .[3]

Not everybody is faced by such a dilemma as Hamlet's, but everyone has to face injustice and misfortune. At certain times in life, anyone might

---

2. Yancey, *Fearfully and Wonderfully Made*, 76.
3. Shakespeare, *Hamlet* Act 3 Scene 1.

declare life to be a "sea of troubles." And yet, at the same time, the person who feels badly treated by life—the person suffering the slings and arrows of outrageous fortune—can still be someone who believes in the love and grace underlying the whole of life. In short, that same person can be a believer in God, and in the underlying reality, an ocean of love.

The sea is also regarded as "a sea of troubles" in Hebrew life and thought. It is considered to be a place to be feared. Its sheer size, its unpredictable storms and its elemental power all make it alarming and hazardous. It was originally thought to contain fearsome creatures such as the Leviathan of the Book of Job. So rather than representing the possibility of freedom, adventure and profitable trade—as for the Phoenicians, for example—it represented for the Jewish people great danger and the unknown. In the Creation narrative of Genesis chapter 1, chaos appears to be a "watery deep," which God has to control. Thus, on the second day of creation, God separates the waters above the firmament from those below, and then on the third day, he gathers together the waters under the sky to separate them from the dry land. This "separating out" means that order is imposed and the waters are kept at bay. The original chaos of waters and wind passing over the face of the deep is overcome and the threat of floods and drowning is minimized.

So life is two-sided—there is an ocean of love underlying all things, and at the same time a sea of troubles threatening life and limb. During the journey of life, we can see marvellous things and be impressed by the signs of God's providence and love. Yet we know that suddenly we can be overtaken by bad luck. Our health might break down, we might lose our job, we might lose our long-term partner. We sometimes have to face great adversity. In a similar way, the oceans and seaways of the world can give rise to a sense of wonder and awe at their beauty and vastness, while at the same time storms and tempests can arise at sea and batter the vessel trying to make its way to a safe haven. So my chosen metaphor for life in this world is like a two-sided coin: an ocean of love and a sea of troubles. They are both aspects of one and the same thing—life with all its risks and dangers, its high adventures, its challenges and trials, its triumphs and delights. In life, as William Blake observed, joy and woe are woven fine.

Joy and woe are indeed woven fine in the life we know in this world. In a notebook now known as The Pickering Manuscript, the poet and visionary,

William Blake wrote a poem called "Auguries of Innocence." It was written in 1803 but never published until 1863, in Alexander Gilchrist's biography of Blake. The poem combines Blake's ideas in his poetry collections *"Songs of Innocence"* and *"Songs of Experience,"* showing how this world, this life, is a strange paradox. On the one hand it is a world full of beauty, harmony, order and splendor. On the other hand, it is a world full of evil, traumas, corruption and suffering. The poem is 112 lines long, and contains this memorable stanza:

> It is right that it should be so;
> Man was made for Joy and Woe;
> And when this we rightly know
> Through the world we safely go.
> Joy and woe are woven fine,
> A clothing for the Soul divine;
> Under every grief and pine
> Runs a joy with silken twine.

William Blake makes us aware that life is bound to be a mixture of enjoyment; even joy—and trouble—or "woe" as he has it. However, interestingly, Blake also regards this inextricable blending together of joy and woe as "a clothing for the soul divine"; as though this combination makes life somehow a higher adventure, a more noble quest—a place where virtues like courage, endurance, tenacity, compassion and care can be developed and perfected. Without this combination of joy and woe, people cannot grow and mature in such virtues or rise to embody them in their lives. Blake also argues in this poem that "grief and pine," as he puts it, do not have the last word. Underneath all suffering there "runs a joy with silken twine."

༄

Rose Schaap, the author of a memoir called *Drinking with Men*[4] tells in her book of how she had a bedtime vision of a lamb with the face of William Blake. Shortly before that vision, she had been studying Blake's poetry and recognized it a call for a better world, for a more imaginative and empathetic way of living. She was impressed with Blake's concern for justice, and his indignation and anger at the way some people were downtrodden and ill-treated.

A while before Rose Schaap had her vision, she underwent a time of grieving for a loved one she had lost. She opened her book of Blake's poetry and read the stanza printed above. The words had a profound effect on her

---

4. Schaap, *Drinking with Men*.

as she meditated and pondered upon them. The poetry did not take away her grief; her loved one was not revived, as she put it, but quietly and imperceptibly, her experience of grief shifted and changed. The passage from Blake seemed to allow her to live in the grief and accept it as part of life, but at the same time, it seemed to indicate that joy would break through; that, entwined with the sadness—which had seemed all-encompassing—there was a golden thread of happiness. Blake did not save her life or change everything, but, as she put it, "he lit a little votive in the small, dark chapel of loss, by whose light I started to see a way through."

It is my conviction that suffering and joy are somehow linked and connected in *all* our experience of life, and so the separating out of suffering, treating it as an undiluted pain or grief, can be true at a certain time, and for a period of time, but is not true all of the time, or for all times. The idea that suffering is *only* loss or pain is not true to our experience of life as a whole.

Nevertheless, the question of suffering constantly stares everybody, and especially religious believers, in the face. It is the most obvious challenge to belief in a loving and all-powerful God. It is also an inescapable fact of human life and touches human beings at the core of their existence. The entire Buddhist religion is built around the idea that the whole of life is, in some sense, continuous effort, strain and suffering. How to react to this and to respond to it is the major question the Buddha himself wrestled with. But this same question has vexed the biblical writers both in the Hebrew Scriptures (the Old Testament) and in the New Testament, and there is a variety of responses to the reality of human suffering in both Testaments.

As far as the Bible is concerned, the problem of suffering is addressed as far back as the eighth century BC, for in the book of Micah, we have the prophet asking the question, "Where is the God of justice?"(2:17). Much later, and in philosophical thought, the early Christian writer Boethius (c. 480– c. 524 AD) raised the same issue with his simple question, "If God is righteous, then why evil?"

However, in this chapter I am not attempting to find a philosophical answer to the question of suffering. This work is not intended to be what the German philosopher and mathematician G. W. F. Leibniz (1646–1716) called a "theodicy"; an attempt to reconcile the idea of a loving and just God with the reality of suffering. Rather the task I envisage is more practically based: first, is there evidence of God's presence and activity in life? Secondly, how have biblical writers responded to suffering?

Then thirdly, how have ordinary people in modern times maintained their faith despite the reality of suffering in their lives?

After some thought and consideration, I have come to the conclusion that most suffering falls into one of three main areas, and I will use an illustration or two to give a more focused idea of each of these areas. The first area is *the suffering caused by human sin:* what used to be called "man's inhumanity to man."

(1) Mikhail Kalashnikov first went to church at the age of 91—yes, at the end of his life—and he was subsequently baptised. He died recently at the grand old age of 94. He was the inventor of the AK47 assault rifle named after him, the Kalashnikov.

After his conversion to Orthodox Christianity, he wrote to the head of the Russian Orthodox Church of his spiritual pain over all the people killed by the weapon he had invented. "Am I guilty of people's deaths, even if they were enemies?" he asked. "The longer I live, the more troubled I am by this question: why does the Lord allow man to have devilish desires of envy, greed and aggression? Why does God allow thoughts of killing and evil to burst out of humankind? Did the Lord really design it so?"

Kalashnikov realized that the killing weapon he had invented was simply the expression of a deeper evil that lurked in the heart of human beings: as he put it—"devilish desires of envy, greed and aggression." It is what the Church calls "sin."

This dark side of human nature is responsible—directly or indirectly—for the greater part of the world's suffering

Originally, Mr. Kalashnikov was motivated by his desire to defend his country, by his pride in its achievements. He was also motivated by an ambition to rise above the dispossessed Siberian peasant status he had been born into. Later in his life, after he had seen the power of his assault rifle and its widespread use in virtually every conflict around the world up to the present day, he was troubled by doubts about what he had enabled people to do to one another. His soul was distressed when he considered child soldiers murdering people in cold blood with the AK47, government troops attacking defenceless civilians with the AK47, rebels murdering government officials with the AK47, criminals perpetrating violent crimes with the AK47, conflicts causing endless suffering to ordinary people because of the AK47. He had given human aggression and lust for revenge a physical incarnation and written it large through the power of his invention. He said near the end of his life: "My spiritual pain is unbearable. I keep having the same unsolved question: if my rifle took away people's lives, can it be that I am guilty of people's deaths?"

☙

Another fine example of the suffering caused by what was called "man's inhumanity to man" is provided by the snapshot of slavery in the southern states of America in the film *Twelve Years a Slave* (2013) directed by Steve McQueen and starring Chiwetei Ejiofor. This film is based on the real life memoirs of Solomon Northup, whose account of his sufferings was published in 1863. It graphically described his kidnapping and the brutal environment of the slave traders and their sadistic treatment of their "property"—the slaves. When people are regarded as "property," they can all too easily be treated with contempt and any dissent be crushed with callous brutality.

(2) My second area under consideration is *the suffering caused by natural disasters or catastrophes*—which are sometimes called in law "Acts of God." On the fourth of September 2010, an earthquake of 7.1 magnitude on the Richter scale struck Christchurch, New Zealand's second largest city, at 4.35 a.m. local time. Aftershocks have continued right up to the present day—in fact, one of them, on the twenty second of February 2011, caused 185 deaths (far more than the original quake). In the earthquake, many buildings were destroyed, power went down, and the Cathedral in Christchurch was so badly damaged, it had to be demolished. Insurance claims from the original earthquake amounted to some three billion NZ dollars. There would have been more injuries and deaths had not most buildings in Christchurch been reinforced and well constructed.

I have chosen this particular example because my nephew Ben, his pregnant wife, Saray, and their first child, Henry, were living in Christchurch at that time. Ben is a surgeon, and he saw many of the worst affected people in the aftermath to the earthquake: those who were seriously injured, those who had to lose limbs, those who were hospitalized. Ben's wife, Saray and her son Henry, were in their home when the earthquake struck: cracks appeared in the walls and the house could easily have collapsed upon them. They took refuge under a wooden table. The family were later evacuated, and Saray, having faced danger and the possibility of death, was somewhat traumatized. But I remember a time later on, when my sister, Ben's mother, asked me, "Why did it happen? How can there be a God if he allows this to happen?" This is the question that troubled the biblical writers and has haunted all Christians and theists ever since.

The same question was asked by the philosopher and writer Voltaire, in the wake of the famous Lisbon earthquake of 1755. It occurred on All Saints Day (November 1st) at a time when thousands of people were attending church services—at around 9.40 in the morning and onwards. The earthquake registered 8.5—9.00 on the Richter scale. It caused most of the buildings in Lisbon to collapse, and subsequent fires and tidal waves almost totally destroyed the city. The death toll is uncertain, but is reckoned between 10,000 and 100,000 souls. Voltaire, in his novel Candide, rejected the easy optimism of his day and the philosopher Leibniz's slogan that "this is the best of all possible worlds." Voltaire had Candide visit Lisbon, experience the earthquake and lie buried for a while underneath the rubble. Voltaire's supporters, the rationalists and "encyclopedistes" of his day, questioned how a benign deity could possible allow such a terrible event to take place.

(3) My third area of focus concerns *the suffering caused by physical illness and mental anguish*. More than four million people with long-term physical health conditions were also found to have significant mental health problems, and many of them experience significantly poor health outcomes and reduced quality of life as a result. Physical and mental health are closely interrelated. I will briefly look at mental health and the concomitant suffering caused by it. In terms of National Health Service spending in the UK, at least £1 in every £8 spent on long-term or chronic conditions is linked to poor mental health and well-being. Some 38% of those who had health problems also had indications of anxiety or depression.

In Australia there is now an Anxiety and Depression Awareness month (October). Apparently, over a million people in Australia live with depression and over 2 million have an anxiety disorder. In USA there is now an Anxiety and Depression week. More than 40 million Americans suffer with an anxiety disorder and over 20 million with some kind of depressive illness. (out of a total population of 300 million). Without even considering the causes of all this we can say that the cost in human suffering is immeasurable.

In the UK, *The Guardian* newspaper of the nineteenth of June 2013 reported the findings of the Mental Health Foundation for the UK, the results of a survey of 40,000 households, conducted between 2010 and 2011. It was then estimated that 1 in 4 of the UK population experience some kind of mental health problems in the course of a year. Anxiety and depression together affect almost 20% of the population (according to the Office for National Statistics). The highest incidence of mild mental illness is in the 50—54 age group. Alarmingly, around 10% of children have mental health problems at any one time. In the population over the age of sixteen, 21% of women and 16% of men are affected by anxiety or depression, and depression affects 1 in 5 of older people. These conditions are most pronounced among those separated or divorced, but high levels are also reported by those who are out of work. *The Guardian* reported that only 1 in 10 of the UK prison population has *no* mental disorder.

Mental distress or illness can have a whole variety of triggers. Some can have more physical causes: drug addiction, alcoholism, homelessness, trauma after bullying or mugging: others can have more emotional or spiritual causes: bereavement, rejection or abandonment, redundancy and loss of purpose or status, personal debt, overwork or pressure at work; tension in relationships, and so it goes on.

Whatever the cause these statistics must give us all pause to stop and ponder. What is wrong with modern life that it causes so much suffering? And this at a time when we can treat physical illnesses so much better than in any previous generation, and when we claim to understand mental illness better than ever before. One thing these alarming figures show is that distress of all kinds is on the increase in western society. It is also clear that the spirit, mind and body are closely connected. With the weakening of religious faith, it appears to be true that people are more prone to anxiety and spiritual depression.

The three areas I have looked at through examples are not my attempt to summarize exhaustively the types of suffering. However, they do cover in general terms the main domains: first, suffering caused by sin and the harmful actions of human beings (which is the major contributor to the suffering in the world); second, the dislocations in the natural world which cause disasters and elemental events such as floods, earthquakes and tsunamis; then thirdly, the suffering caused by physical illness, mental pain, spiritual unease and depression.

CHAPTER TWO

FOUNDATIONS

THE MATERIALIST UNDERSTANDING OF reality is somewhat "flat" and lacking in depth. On the other hand, a spiritual view of reality allows for mysteries and hidden profundities. If we were materialists, we might imagine reality like a lot of objects placed on a table; but the table-top is the underlying hard surface we cannot go beneath. Our knowledge of reality is thus limited to solid objects—the table top and all that lies upon it. Another similar example might be that of a billiard table with balls moving about on the surface. This would be a more mobile universe, but the green baize is like space—dense but impenetrable. The same restrictions apply to material reality as in the first example.

However, an alternative conception of reality would be to regard sense data as what we can see and touch etc., but to accept that there is a great deal lying beyond our purview: hidden atomic nuclei, electrons whirling in space, quantum events—but more space than anything else. Beyond these visible events there are invisible forces—electro-magnetism, gravity, light waves, weak and strong nuclear forces. And as space in this scenario is essentially "open," beyond all that again there could be spiritual powers and invisible presences . . . This latter view of reality is much closer to the "true" and "scientific" understanding of reality today.

The materialist view, so much favoured by nineteenth century positivists, still lingers in the work of logical positivists (for whom all talk of "God" is transcendental and therefore unknowable or unverifiable). Other modern atheist apologists seem to retain this "flat" and impenetrable view of reality. Even if they accept realities beyond the data of our senses, these are only in the form of further "material" universes and other "dimensions" linked to space-time, which have nothing to do with spiritual powers.

In all that follows, the hidden depths of reality are assumed and explored. Poets have always looked at the world in new ways and have probed and scrutinized the nature of things in such a way as to get beneath mere appearances to the deeper truths buried below all superficial apprehension. In his poem *"God's grandeur"* Gerard Manley Hopkins wrote about the deeper levels of reality beneath—but permeating—surface impressions:

> The world is charged with the grandeur of God.
> It will flame out, like shining from shook foil;
> It gathers to a greatness, like the ooze of oil,
> Crushed . . .
>
> Nature is never spent;
> There lies the dearest freshness deep down things;
> And though the last lights off the black West went
> Oh! Morning, at the brown brink eastward, springs –
> Because the Holy Ghost over the bent
> World broods with warm breast and with ah! bright wings.[1]

1. Science and Faith: Is Faith Rational?

Faith has been much under attack recently from a new militant atheism, represented by Richard Dawkins, Christopher Hitchens, Sam Harris, Daniel Dennett, A.C. Grayling and others. The central plank of their attack is that faith and science do not mix and are very different—and competing—ways of interpreting life, the Universe and everything.

The atheist argument goes that science gives a rational explanation of the way things are (reality), whereas faith is irrational and constitutes a "leap in the dark." But this has not traditionally been the accepted scholarly view. In the medieval period, the Church often encouraged scientific research, and scholars like Robert Grosseteste and Copernicus were able to follow their research wherever it led them. The persecution of Galileo was the exception rather than the rule. Then, in the seventeenth century science and faith were close companions, especially in the Protestant world. Isaac

---

1. Manley, *Selected Poems*, 114.

Newton believed that his mathematical and scientific work would uncover and reveal much about the rational way God had created the Universe.

Towards the end of the twentieth century it looked as though science and religion were drawing closer together, and, if not becoming reconciled, at least having their own discrete domains and methods. Science was seen as describing the nature of reality and its laws: faith was seen as asking questions about meaning and probing into the ethical and spiritual realms. So where science might attempt to describe what happened in the first few seconds of the BIG BANG at the beginning of time, faith would be interested in asking what it implied for the Universe to have a beginning, a moment of creation; why it came into being (purpose) and why it had beauty and harmony within it.

The new atheists appear to have failed to understand faith on at least two counts. Firstly, faith is in fact empirically and rationally based. Nobody believes in God for no good reason. Belief is the result of reflection upon life and upon the nature of reality. Secondly, the God of faith is not entirely transcendent and unknowable. The Christian God is both immanent –active in the world—*and* transcendent—that is, going beyond the limits of life as we know it.

The rationality of the Universe has some of the features that follow:

(i) The Universe must be intelligible for us to know it and comprehend it at all.

If it behaved irrationally and randomly all the time—as one would expect of a Universe which came about entirely by chance—then no one could grasp its laws or make predictions about how it will behave in the future. Further, it has been an amazing discovery to some scientists; for example, Professor Michael Heller—a recent winner of the Templeton Prize—that the Universe can be rendered understandable by mathematical models. In other words, the Universe can be matched to the ultimate rational template—a series of equations. Professor Paul Davies wrote: "Somehow the Universe has engineered, not only its own awareness, but its own comprehension. Mindless, blundering atoms have conspired to make, not just *life*, not just *mind*, but *understanding*." Davies goes on to say that the Greek philosophers" great contribution to human knowledge, was that they "encouraged the belief that the world could be explained by logic, reasoning and mathematics." He then quotes the astronomer, James Jeans: "The Universe appears to have been designed by a pure mathematician.[2]

2. *The Goldilocks Enigma*, 5, 6, and 9.

The implication of this idea is that equations can be written down that capture or model the real world of experience in a mathematical world of numbers and algebraic formulae. Then, by manipulating these mathematical symbols, someone could work out what will happen in the real world, without actually carrying out the observation.

This is exactly what takes place when a space rocket is sent to Mars . . . Scientists can calculate exactly when the capsule will reach the red planet; the speed it needs to travel at, the precise time at which it needs to be launched to coincide with Mars's orbit; how much fuel it will need, the precise trajectory of both the capsule and the planet; the position of earth in relation to Mars at the time of the launch, and so on and so forth.

Even Shakespeare, in his epic poem, *Troilus and Cressida*, recognized the order in heaven and earth:

> The heavens themselves, the planets and this center,
> Observe degree, priority and place,
> Insisture, course, proportion, season, form,
> Office and custom, in all line of order.[3]

⸻

(ii) The Universe seems to have been designed so that it is "just right for life."

This idea is what Paul Davies calls "The Goldilocks Enigma" and forms the main subject of his book of that name. Davies shows that there are an astonishing number of "coincidences" which must occur, *and occur together*, for the Universe itself to emerge and for life to emerge from it.

Here are a few examples:

Right at the beginning of creation, matter and anti-matter were formed in almost equal amounts. In a millisecond of time the Universe cooled enough for quarks and anti-quarks to "condense out." If a quark met an anti-quark, they would cancel each other out. An exact symmetry would seem to be the most likely outcome. But in fact for every billion quarks and anti-quarks, there was one extra quark! That infinitesimal fraction of potential served to make up the entire Universe as we know it!

If there had been exact symmetry, the Universe would have ended in pure radiation and no galaxies, stars or planets could have formed.

Second, the expansion of the Universe in the first moments of the Big Bang took its mass from a microscopic but almost infinitely dense mass to a

---

3. Shakespeare, *Troilus and Cressida*, Act 1 Scene 3.

vast and almost infinite extension. Space was thus created and time began! This is mind-boggling in itself. The entire Universe was contained in a mass smaller than a golf ball!

But *the rate* of that expansion was critical. It required very precise fine-tuning. Prof. Stephen Hawkins wrote: "Why did the Universe start out at so nearly the critical rate of expansion that separates models that re-collapse from those that go on expanding forever? If the rate of expansion had been smaller by ONE PART in one hundred thousand million million, the Universe would have collapsed back on itself. On the other hand, if the rate or speed of expansion had been greater by even ONE PART IN A MILLION, stars and planets would not have had time or gravity to form."

Thirdly, the formation of "heavy elements" is also remarkable. If the "strong" nuclear force that holds protons and neutrons together had been very slightly weaker, only hydrogen could have formed in the Universe. On the other hand, if the "strong" nuclear force had been very slightly stronger, all the hydrogen would have turned into helium. The combination that we actually have—a quarter helium to three quarters hydrogen—is exactly what is required to generate heavier elements in the nuclear reactions and fusions taking place in the heart of (the first) stars. The *carbon* necessary for life could not have been formed without this incredibly fine tuning.

The same incredible "coincidences" occur with the other two elemental forces in the Universe—electromagnetism and gravity. Francis Collins, in his book, *The Language of God,* writes, "The chance that all of these constants would take on the values necessary to result in a stable Universe capable of sustaining complex life forms is infinitesimal . . . In sum, our Universe is wildly improbable"[4]

All this is known as "The Anthropic Principle."

How do the "new atheists" respond to this? Either they insist that these coincidences are a happy chance. OR they assert that our Universe is one of millions of parallel Universes and happens to be the one which has the characteristics capable of bringing forth life as we know it.

Although the idea of parallel Universes has gained wide currency among scientists in recent years, it seems to me that is an un-testable theory. If we apply a verification principle, then the multiple Universe idea fails at the first hurdle, because it is essentially *a metaphysical theory*; that is, one which goes beyond the bounds of the observable and the empirical. This failure to meet any criterion of experimental testing is exactly what atheist scientists accuse religious people of. They argue that the hypothesis of God is un-testable, unverifiable and metaphysical.

---

4. Collins, *Language of God,* 74.

In fact, that accusation is in large measure untrue, because God's existence can be inferred from signs of God's activity in the world. For instance, the creation of an orderly, rationally understandable Universe would seem only to be explicable by the action of a divine intelligence. This is the conclusion arrived at by Professor Anthony Flew. He was a long-time atheist philosopher; famous for his masterwork, *An Introduction to Western Philosophy*—a very popular introductory text for University courses. But his final book took his supporters by surprise. It is entitled *There is a God: How the world's most notorious atheist changed his mind*; and in it Flew argues that the Universe displays so many features of rational creativity that there must be an intelligent creator behind it all!

Returning to the idea of multiple parallel Universes—the theory seems to me to fail another test—the one known as "Ockham's razor," whereby the simplest and most elegant explanation is regarded as the most probably correct one. This thesis derives from Willlian of Ockham, a medieval scholastic philosopher. The idea of an infinite number of Universes to explain how this one—eminently suited to bring forth life forms—came into being, seems unnecessarily complicated. On the other hand, the idea of a divine intelligence creating the right conditions for life despite almost impossible odds—that is the simple explanation, and satisfies the demands of "Ockham's razor."

(iii) The Universe should have zero mass.

Up until very recently scientists faced a very great and awkward puzzle. Examining the "weak" nuclear force in the Universe and in particular, the symmetries controlling its interactions, the Universe should have zero mass. In other words, it should be an unformed chaos of scattered elementary particles with nothing to draw them together. The British theoretical physicist, Peter Higgs, along with his team of scientists, therefore posited the necessity of a particular particle which had the power to bestow mass upon all the other elementary particles; so that "solid" materials and dense substances could be formed. For fifty years, many scientists searched for the Higgs particle or Higgs boson, but to no avail. However, with the building of the Large Hadron Collider (CERN) in Switzerland, a facility became available which could separate out elementary particles and "photograph" them, even if their existence were momentary.

The discovery and isolation of the mysterious quantum particle known as the Higgs Boson would confirm the hypothesis put forward by Peter Higgs to explain the reality of *objects with mass* in our Universe. The almost magical power of the Higgs particle earned it the nickname of "The

God particle," because if it existed it made possible the formation of stars, planets, meteors, comets and asteroids—in fact, all objects of substance in the Universe. On the fourth of July 2012, scientists at the Large Hadron Collider finally announced that they could demonstrate the existence of the Higgs Boson. There was great excitement throughout the world. The mechanism or facility for the creation of matter was now *verifiable* as a quantum field containing the elementary particle which conferred mass on all other elementary particles.

Nevertheless, there is a dark side to the Higgs Boson. It enables black holes to form in the Universe: in other words, the mass of a certain area could become so dense that gravity would draw everything around it into its unbreakable grip. Entire solar systems—even galaxies in the long run—could be sucked into the irresistible pull of the black hole. Not even light waves could escape from its intense gravity; which means that black holes cannot even be "seen" from space. Because no light emerges from a black hole, we cannot ascertain what exactly is inside it.

However, an even more recent discovery—on the eleventh of February 2016—has opened up the possibility of a new way of "mapping" the Universe. That discovery was that of gravitational "waves"—detected around black holes. These "waves" mean that gravity can actually be observed and measured. That in turn means that a new way of picturing or perceiving the Universe is now conceivable. Gravity waves give a new perspective on the Universe.

These discoveries not only give us cause to marvel at the properties and wonders of the Universe, but they demonstrate that in the cosmos there are forces which work together to make possible the very existence of space and time, mass and matter. The probability of this being mere coincidence again seems highly problematic, not to say almost impossible. It is not good enough simply to say that our Universe just happens to have all the right qualities, for existence and for the emergence of life forms. The "coincidences" and creative activities involved need explaining.

To sum up, the Universe displays an incredible working together of the many forces and properties which allow it to exist in the first place. It also displays a regularity and order that allow for repeated scientific experiments. If a scientist could not perform an experiment more than once under exactly the same conditions and expect the same result, then no progress could possibly be made in understanding the nature of reality. Most people of faith understand—or at least sense—the order and harmony underlying everyday reality; even if they have not investigated the science.

Now if we turn to the Bible and take a look at Genesis chapter 1—the Creation story—we discover that this is not intended to be a scientific account per se. Nevertheless, it does lay down certain principles about life, which could be interpreted as scientific. For instance, light is seen to be the initial act of creation. And in fact, scientists regard light as the fundamental energy source of the Universe. Secondly, God's role in creation is seen as bringing order out of chaos. In other words, God imposes rational organization onto a primeval "formless void." He separates light from darkness; then he divides the waters above the firmament (rain) from those below (seas and rivers); next, he separates the waters from the dry land; and then he is able to concentrate on bringing into being all the abundant varieties of life on earth. This is a story about a God who likes everything to find its rightful place.

One other aspect of the Creation story is worth mentioning; namely, the fact that all things are regarded as interconnected. The plants and trees depend upon the sun and the waters for their life; the animals and birds depend upon the plants, berries and seeds for their food—at this stage, animals and humans appear to be vegetarian! Part of the purpose of the light and the darkness is to give balance to life. All creatures are able to act energetically for part of their life, and rest and gain refreshment and renewal during another part. Human beings benefit from having both light and darkness to provide work time and time for rest.

The fact that all things are interconnected finds its echo in scientific research as well. The film *"The theory of everything"* (2015) has as its centerpiece the search by scientist Stephen Hawkins for a simple and elegant theorem, which can express how the whole of life operates and depends upon a few basic laws. This theorem remains somewhat elusive, but Einstein's General Theory of Relativity has certainly proved beyond doubt that time, space and mass are intimately linked and bound together, and that the laws of physics are reliable to a large degree. The problem is when the infinitesimally small—the quantum world—meets the easily observable Universe. The same laws do not apply. Or again, when an object is travelling close to the speed of light, mass and other properties change and create new conditions, governed by laws unlike those of Newton. Nevertheless, scientists do regard all the aspects of the known Universe as so closely interconnected that "a theory of everything" is a possibility. When we stop to think about it, this is a remarkable fact. Why should all things be connected? Why should time and space be affected by mass or vice versa? A random Universe should surely be composed of random elements, all "doing their own thing" without any necessary bond or unity between all the different aspects. The interweaving and intertwining of all things seem to bespeak intelligent creation rather than arbitrary occurrences.

The Book of Proverbs teaches that the world came into being not only through orderly planning, but with *wisdom* at the heart of it. In Proverbs chapter 8 "Lady Wisdom" declares: "The Lord created me at the beginning of his work; the first of his acts of long ago. Ages ago, I was set up, at the first, before the beginning of the earth . . . When he established the heavens I was there, when he drew a circle on the face of the deep, when he made firm the skies above, when he established the fountains of the deep, when he assigned to the sea its limit . . . when he marked out the foundations of the earth, then I was beside him, like a master worker, and I was daily his delight, rejoicing before him always, rejoicing in his inhabited world, and delighting in the human race" (vv. 22–23; 27–31). In Proverbs the main task of humankind is therefore to discover or rediscover the wisdom that lies below the surface of things: the wisdom of the way the world has been created; the wisdom of how to live a good life, the wisdom of how to maintain good relations with others, the wisdom of how to make good decisions, the wisdom of how to find God.

2. Why is the World Beautiful?

The final act of God at the end of each of the days of creation is to pronounce his creation to be "good." Despite the fact that the world is flawed and spoiled in many ways, at the same time it is recognized as fundamentally beautiful—full of marvelous uplifting vistas, patterns, and harmonious shapes. We only need to think of the panoramic view of a mountain range, the gorgeous colors of a winter sunset or the sun's glory at the break of dawn. Then there are the Great Wall of China, the Niagara Falls and the Great Rift Valley, the Rocky Mountains and the Grand Canyon.

We only need to think of the pattern of the snowflake—each one different from all the others; the glory of each flower and plant; the majesty of the trees; the beauty of an icicle or of an underground cave. And of course the ocean is also a beautiful sight, with its wide horizons, its blue-gray color, its ebb and flow, its waves and foaming water.

Even man-made creations can reflect the beauty of creation in general: the Taj Mahal, Notre Dame Cathedral in Paris or St. Paul's in London, the Eiffel Tower, the New York skyline; the Terracotta Army, Sydney Opera House; the great works of art in numerous galleries around the world: all of these inspire a sense of awe and uplift us with their beautiful proportions.

The poet William Blake was able to see beauty in the tiniest things—a grain of sand, a wild flower:

To see a world in a grain of sand
and a heaven in a wild flower
Hold infinity in the palm of your hand
and eternity in an hour.[5]

Elizabeth Barrett-Browning, another nineteenth century poet, wrote in her long poem *Aurora Leigh*, "Earth's crammed with heaven / And every common bush afire with God / but only he who sees, takes off his shoes / The rest sit round it and eat blackberries." It is only those who take time to contemplate and reflect upon the world who see beyond the mundane and the superficial. And indeed, the beauty of the world is hidden from those who choose not to notice. The cell biologist Ursula Goodenough wrote in her book, *The Sacred Depths of Nature* that "the beauty of Nature—sunsets, woodlands, fireflies—has elicited religious emotions through the ages. We are moved to awe and wonder at the grandeur, the poetry, the richness of natural beauty: it fills us with joy and thanksgiving."[6] And this was written by a person who rejects traditional religion. So creation has radiance and beauty, but it is open to interpretation. Some would see all of it as a splendid sign of or pointer to God; others would just regard it as simply the wonderful way the world is.

Scientists can be strongly motivated in their work by the perception that there is a beauty in what they are studying. Ruth Bancewicz, herself a research biologist, writes in her book, *God in the Lab*: "A scientist may find beauty in the objects they study—the data—whether that is a group of organisms, a diagnostic printout, or an aesthetically pleasing series of molecules. I've given some examples of this in biology, but chemists also enjoy this sort of beauty, as do astronauts. I'm sure that researchers in most fields of science find at least some of their data beautiful."[7] A little later in the same chapter she goes on to say, "Scientists enjoy beauty in the same way that we enjoy the serenity of a garden or carefully tended olive grove on a summer's day. Bringing order from chaos, watching things develop and become chaotic again and bringing order once more using reason, creativity and imagination, is one of the most fulfilling experiences in life. The startling elegance of the mathematical solution, or the model that makes sense of what seemed to be a muddle of data is . . . not only attractive, but it is also deeply satisfying."[8]

---

5. Blake, *Songs of Innocence and Songs of Experience*.
6. Quoted in Bancewicz, *God in the Lab*, 137.
7. Ibid., 133.
8. Ibid., 154.

It is true to say then that the symmetry, pattern, and intricate detail we apprehend in and through experiences of the world is the result of finely balanced physical properties. Natural phenomena, including insects and animals, are symmetrical because the laws underlying their creation and formation are symmetrical.

⁓

In Psalm 19 in the Bible, we read the words: "The heavens are telling the glory of God, and the firmament proclaims his handiwork" (v. 1). Then, mysteriously, we read, "Day to day pours forth speech, and night to night declares knowledge" (v. 2). The psalmist appears to be saying that, without words and soundlessly (see v. 3) the creation reveals itself as the work of God, and that this is seen through its radiance and glory. Two other biblical Psalms, which reflect on the glories of Creation, dwell a great deal on the fact that God's work is beautiful. These are Psalm 104 and Psalm 139. Unlike the prose account of creation in Genesis 1, these psalms attempt to express the beauty of creation through the use of poetry. So the greatness of God the creator is linked to his created works:

> You are clothed with honor and majesty,
> wrapped in light as with a garment.
> You stretch out the heavens like a tent,
> You set the beams of your chambers on the waters,
> You make the clouds your chariot,
> You ride on the wings of the wind.
> You make the winds your messengers,
> Fire and flame your ministers.

This psalm goes on to examine various different aspects of the created order: the earth itself established on firm foundations, the springs and rivers coursing their way to the sea, the fertility of the soil providing food for animals and humans, the majesty of the trees and the great rock formations, the elemental power of the ocean with its monsters and teeming forms of life. This psalm is not only a demonstration of God's creativity and power; it is a celebration of God's love of beauty and desire to multiply wonderful and attractive forms of life.

Psalm 139 explores a different aspect of God's creation: the way in which the human being is "fearfully and wonderfully made" (v. 14). It describes God's involvement in our creation even before we are conceived. Even in the womb God is active: "You form my inward parts; you knit me together in my mother's womb" (v. 13). Even before our existence, God is aware of what he intends us to be and how our life will come into being. So the psalmist constantly moves into praise: "How weighty are your thoughts, O God! How vast the sum of them! I try to count them—they are more than the sand" (vv. 17–18). This psalm is a celebration of God's creation on the microscopic scale, whereas Psalm 104 contemplates the vast, the great, and the magnificent. The attention God pays to the tiniest detail of life—rendering it beautiful—is as much a marvel as the attention he pays to the grand gesture and the sweeping grandeur of life.

⁓

Music also has its own grandeur and glory, and can also be intricate and perfect in its detail. It also has patterns and proportions, which can be demonstrated by mathematical formulae. The Ancient Greek mathematician and philosopher, Pythagoras, said, "There is geometry in the humming of the strings; there is music in the spacing of the spheres." Pythagoras used numerical terms to express the intervals between notes, and believed that music which sounds ordered or pleasant is music which expresses mathematical relationships. Thus, for example, the octave of any pitch refers to a frequency exactly twice that of the given pitch. Succeeding super-octaves are then pitches found at frequencies four, eight, sixteen times and so on, of the fundamental frequency. The ratios between notes can therefore be expressed in terms of mathematical intervals.

Researchers at the Universities of Stanford (USA) and McGill (Canada) analyzed almost two thousand musical compositions by different composers of different centuries, and uncovered a mathematical formula governing the *rhythmic patterns* in music (i.e. the timings of rhythms). This formula is based on the discovery that *fractal patterns* appear and reappear in musical compositions just as they do in the forms of snowflakes, fern fronds and broccoli florets! J.S. Bach used fractal symmetry in his compositions quite extensively, especially in the fugues, where the theme is repeated in different ways many times. This can be understood as an interplay of themes and harmonies interweaving and criss-crossing. Now, because the notes and themes relate to each other in mathematical proportions, they interact without ever sounding discordant or "wrong." In fact, they display an intricate beauty.

The ways in which musical compositions reflect the patterns and especially the symmetries of the Universe go some way to explaining why they appeal to us humans as *beautiful* creations. Music is not only mathematical, but is harmonious and euphonious and is capable of striking a chord with our innermost feelings and emotions. We can be uplifted, soothed, excited, aroused by music in a way that almost defies rational explanation. But the way we can "tune in" to the harmonies of the created world goes some way towards providing an understanding of the power of music. So music is a potent example of our response to *beauty* in life.

⁌

The great Roman Catholic theologian Hans Urs von Balthasar wrote a multi-volume work entitled *The Glory of the Lord*. This is a work of aesthetics and its main aim is to demonstrate—through a theological consideration of the nature of life—that beauty (i.e. order, pattern, symmetry, harmony, inter-connectedness) reveals the reality of God's presence in his creation. What does this mean? It attempts to show that God's radiance and glory—partly hidden but often glimpsed in our world—shines through the created order and seems to lie just beyond our grasp of everyday practical realities, just as the order and harmony that a scientist sees through the microscope similarly lies just beyond the normal perception of our senses. The Old Testament idea that no one can look on God and live seems to indicate that we grasp God only indirectly and partially. His glory, splendor, majesty, brilliance are partly hidden from us—by the fact that a great deal of what we "see" is not glorious or uplifting, and by the fact that much of the time we are preoccupied with the practicalities of life and do not reflect on what lies just beyond the initial evidence of our senses.

Alistair McGrath gives us pause for thought. He accepts that the heavens are indeed "telling the glory of God," and that "something of God can be known through them." But he goes on to say that "it does not automatically follow from this that *human beings,* situated as we are within nature, are capable unaided . . . of perceiving the divine through the natural order."[9] McGrath argues that creation is not God and therefore does not clearly reveal God's character or purpose. We humans are not perfect and can easily draw the wrong conclusions from an analysis of the created order. And most importantly, the apostle Paul describes the creation as "groaning" is "subject to frustration" and is "in bondage to decay" (Romans 8:20–22). The world we live in is far from perfect and will only reveal God more fully when it is "liberated" and "redeemed" at the end of time.

We should accept this cautionary note, but not regard it as a counsel of despair. We can see enough of God's glory in creation to come to the conclusion that this is the work of God. As Paul also said in Romans 1: "What can be known about God is plain to them [i.e. human beings], because God has shown it to them. Ever since the creation of the world his eternal power and divine nature, invisible though they are, have been understood and seen

---

9. McGrath, *The Open Secret*, 1–2.

through the things he has made" (vv. 19–20). This could hardly be more clearly put and runs counter to the pessimistic and Calvinistic view of the creation as fatally flawed and "fallen." The more positive view of Hans Urs von Balthasar is encouraged by Paul's justification of natural theology.

⁓

There is a final word to add to all that has been said already. Beauty—although very important in our appreciation of life—does not seem to have any point or usefulness in terms of evolutionary theory. How does an appreciation of beauty help a species to adapt to its environment, discover food, relate to the community, or find ways to reproduce? Surely this presents a difficult problem for the evolutionary biologist who would like to contend that the evolutionary process gives a complete and sufficient account of the way the world is and the way it progresses. The fact of an "unnecessary" surplus of beauty—the perception of harmony, order, grace, radiance, etc., in the Universe—is not easily explicable in terms of usefulness, practicality, and application to evolutionary theory. However, it can be readily understood as the revelation—even if only partial—of the creator's hand in his creation.

Having said that, an objection might be raised; that in fact there *is* an evolutionary use for the development of beauty. Plants need to attract bees in order to spread their pollen and to propagate the species; animals need to attract a mate and for them a colorful display or a striking pattern might well serve to attract the attention of the opposite sex. That is certainly true enough, but it only accounts for a small proportion of the beauty discernible in the Universe. The beauty of a photograph showing the Milky Way galaxy or the outer reaches of the Universe is beautiful, but not useful in any evolutionary sense. The same can be said of the sight of the earth from the moon, or the vista of a distant mountain range, or the view of a lake with trees and flowers around its borders. All these images, and many others, highlight the fact that beauty is something "built into" the nature of the Universe and is not only there for a practical purpose.

Another objection might be raised; namely, that beauty is subjective. It is "in the eye of the beholder," and what might appear beautiful to one person might just appear to be a random collection of colors of shapes to another. Maybe there is something in this, but the Universe displays symmetry, pattern, order, proportion, elegance, color, interesting relationships between shapes and so on and seems to speak of much more than a subjective feeling in the mind of an individual. It speaks of a creation which cries out to be appreciated, admired, and treasured.

⁓

3. Wonder and Surprise

In Tolstoy's great novel *War and Peace* one of the heroes, Prince Andrei Bolkonsky enlists in the army and after some time is involved in the war against Napoleon. He fights at the battle of Austerlitz, where the Austrian and Russian armies suffer a heavy defeat. Prince Andrei is injured on the battlefield and falls to the ground. As he lies prostrate, on his back, the sound and fury, the bloodshed and carnage suddenly seem to fade away, and the prince, contemplating his own death, is surprised and astonished by the immensity of the sky:

> "What's this? Am I falling? My legs are giving way," he thought, and fell on his back. He opened his eyes, hoping to see how the struggle between the Frenchmen and the gunners ended . . . But he saw nothing. Above him there was now only the sky—the lofty sky, not clear yet still immeasurably lofty, with gray clouds creeping softly across it. "How quiet, peaceful and solemn! Quite different from when I was running," thought Prince Andrei. "Quite different from us running and shouting and fighting. Not at all like the gunner and the Frenchman dragging the mop from one another with frightened, frantic faces. How differently do these clouds float across that lofty, limitless sky! How was it that I did not see that sky before? And how happy I am to have found it at last! Yes, all is vanity, all is delusion except these infinite heavens. There is nothing, nothing but that. But even it does not exist; there is nothing but peace and stillness. Thanks be to God" (vol. 1, 326).

It is worth quoting this passage at length, because it conveys so well the way in which the world can surprise us by throwing up something unexpected and amazing. And Prince Andrei is very much ready to appreciate this, because of the contrast between the brutality and noise of war and the tranquillity of the heavens above. He suddenly realizes that war is not glorious; the sky is glorious—and it fills him with a sense of wonder. This sense even goes beyond immediate apprehension; for it is almost a religious experience. He glimpses the peace and serenity lying beyond all things; the wonder and beauty of creation. And so the passage ends with "Thanks be to God." Prince Andrei's life is materially affected as well, because before enlisting in the army, he lost his wife in childbirth and then had a period of depression, during which he did not care whether he lived or died. Even at Austerlitz, he made himself a target by picking up the Russian standard and running with it into the thick of the battle. After his injury and his experience of wonder, his life took a turn for the better and he was able to fall in love again and find meaning in his existence.

Now of course it is not always the case that when we are surprised by something wonderful that we then have a deep experience of the harmony and grace of life. Often the sense of wonder is just that—a surprise at something elegant, something lovely, something unexpected and delightful. Richard Dawkins, whilst a vociferous unbeliever, has written a good deal about this sense of wonder, particularly in his books *Unweaving the Rainbow* and *River out of Eden*. Dawkins recognizes that for most people, for most of the time, "there is an anaesthetic of familiarity, a sedative of ordinariness, which dulls the senses and hides the wonder of existence." He goes on to say that, on the other hand, "we can recapture that sense of having just tumbled out to life on a new world by looking at our own world in unfamiliar ways."[10]

The sense of wonder was viewed with suspicion in the Age of Enlightenment—the eighteenth century. It was regarded as an ignorant and irrational response to the data of our senses. Whilst pure reason could explain experience coolly and objectively, reacting with wonder was tantamount to giving way to emotionalism and sentimentality. However, with the rise of the Romantic movement at the end of the eighteenth century and in the early nineteenth, wonder came once again to be seen positively—as an imaginative and creative response to experience. In fact, it was a way to reclaim the childlike innocence of first sight and immediate sensation. John Keats wrote in his poem *Lamia* that science "unweaves the rainbow" and he added, "Do not all charms fly at the mere touch of cold philosophy?" For Keats and the romantic poets, having a sense of wonder about everything was the way to new knowledge and appreciation of life.

We could go even further than Keats and assert, with theologian Jurgen Moltmann, that "reality is always more surprising than we are capable of imagining." As Ruth Bancewicz states; "Even the simplest-looking organism is incredibly complex on the inside."[11] She describes looking at a zebra fish, with its virtually transparent body, and recounts how she had a sense of wonder watching the inner organs at work and the fish enabling itself to move through the water. She then concludes, "Wonder is the stepping stone on the way to awe."[12] She characterizes "awe" as the feeling "when we come across things that are larger, more beautiful, more powerful or complex than anything we see in our everyday lives. To be awestruck is one of the most basic human experiences. The night sky, vast landscapes or the mighty

---

10. Dawkins, *Unweaving the Rainbow*, 6–7.
11. Bancewicz, *God in the Lab*, 159.
12. Ibid., 161.

forces of wind and sea are accessible to almost every person on earth, and can affect us deeply."[13]

An even better example of this feeling of awe is found in the reaction of the two American astronauts who landed on the moon, Neil Armstrong and Buzz Aldrin. It was July 20th and 21st, 1969. As they looked back at their home planet Earth from the moon, they saw a blue sphere floating in the blackness of infinite space. It was an experience of awe for them. They realized how fragile and stunningly beautiful the planet was and how we humans should value it and take great care of it. Buzz Aldrin's response to this was to give thanks to God and to stage a service of Holy Communion.

Some years after the Moon landings, the Hubble Space Telescope, created by the US Space Agency NASA, was launched into orbit in 1990. At first it had problems with a reflecting mirror that was slightly out of focus. This was successfully repaired in space in 1993, and since then the Hubble has recorded some of the most detailed visible-light images of the cosmos. It has also revolutionized our knowledge; in particular enabling astrophysicists to calculate the rate of expansion of the Universe. More than that, it has taken images of the outer reaches of space that have stunned the world with their strangeness and their wonder. These photos show stars forming in pictures that have taken 13.4 billion light years to reach Earth. As such, these are photos of the dawn of the Universe, soon after the "Big Bang." In the future, new telescopes, such as the James Webb Space Telescope (due 2018) and the WFIRST-AFTA mission, scheduled for the mid-2020s, promise to make even more startling and awe-inspiring discoveries.

⸺

The curiosities of the animal kingdom have always given rise to a sense of wonder. There are, firstly, animals which work together for mutual benefit, acting as though they already *know* what the other species requires from them. There are plover birds which pick the teeth of crocodiles, so that they gain food while the crocodiles have their teeth cleaned and irritating food particles removed. There are egrets which sit on the back of elephants or buffalo, picking off and feeding on insects and parasites, thus keeping the larger animal healthy while gaining a meal for themselves. Or again, there are zebras and ostriches which graze side by side, so that each can warn the other of approaching danger. The ostriches have enhanced eyesight, while the zebra have excellent hearing.

Think of the camouflage animals and fish have developed. There are octopi which can mimic nearly twenty other species to ward off different

13. Ibid.

kinds of predators; there are insects that look just like leaves and fish that resemble plants on the sea floor. Some animals can even change shape or color, like the famous chameleon, and blend in with their surroundings and hide from their attackers.

Some animals display remarkable building abilities, and often work in a team to cooperate on big projects. Termites are hard-working insects; creating huge hills as homes for a whole colony, with interlocking tunnels, hatcheries, water reserves and fungal gardens for food production! Weaver birds in South Africa build a battery of nests all under the same thatch and these often accommodate several hundred birds. The communal home offers buffering from extremes of temperature and protection against predators. Or again, bees can build honeycombs which are the ideal shape to economise labor and yet to create an extremely strong and sound structure.

The migration of birds has—from time immemorial—been a source of wonder and speculation. The Arctic Tern is the greatest traveller, flying between breeding grounds in the Arctic to a new home in the Antarctic every year—a distance of some ten to eleven thousand miles. Manx Shearwaters migrate almost nine thousand miles between their northern breeding grounds and the southern ocean. Birds migrate using astronomical guides, the earth's magnetic field and, most probably, memory maps. Whichever method is employed, they can return to the same forest or lake—even the same nest—as they lived in before, pinpointing their destination with uncanny accuracy. The Book of Jeremiah even comments on this as a wonder of God's creation: "Even the stork in the heavens knows its seasons, and the turtle dove, the swift and the crane keep the time of their arrival" (Jer 8:7). Some eighteen hundred of the world's ten thousand bird species are long-distance migrants.

The simple egg, used in reproduction by so many species, is a wonder of nature. It contains the yolk, which furnishes a cradle for the life of the embryo, and albumen surrounding the yolk, which provides food for the growing life inside. And then the shell gives protection and holds in the warmth—essential qualities for the emergence of new life.

The chrysalis, equipping a hidden "home" or sanctuary for the dowdy caterpillar, then allows it to be transformed into a fragile, delicate and colorful butterfly, which takes wing and flies. A quite astonishing change, not only in form, but in function too. It is not surprising that this has been seen as a model of death and resurrection.

These phenomena can be "explained" by evolutionary developments, but underlying such incredible behavior there is still a mystery. How do animals know in advance how to benefit another species and themselves? How do animals and fish develop camouflage even if they *want* to hide by merging with the background? How do they get the body to change its color, texture or shape? What drives insects or birds to build ideal homes for a whole colony? What satellite guidance system in a bird's brain can enable it to find the same nest it had before after a flight of some thousands of miles? What allows a caterpillar to alter its nature and take to the air? These questions are not easy to answer and are rightly considered to be wonders of the natural world.

Sometimes mere statistics can give rise to a sense of wonder—even of awe. And this can be on a microscopic or a macroscopic scale. Allow me to give a few examples of each:

First, at the microscopic level. The copying of the DNA double helix in our bodies takes place at the rate of 670,000 sub-units every minute. On average, in a chain of ten thousand million copies of the necessary code, just *one mistake* is made. Thus, DNA replication is incredibly accurate and, at the same time, incredibly rapid.

In our bodies we have so many strands of DNA that if they were all placed end to end, they would reach to the sun and back three hundred times over (186 million miles x 300). That is 55,800,000,000 miles.

Another example concerns the generation of energy in our bodies. The breaking down of carbohydrates, fats, and proteins in the process of digestion surely gives rise *in itself* to a sense of wonder. Through the action of stomach acids and different chemical reactions, the body appears to *"know"* which parts of our food it should retain and use to maintain our bodies and their energy, and which parts to reject and jettison. Large quantities of a simple molecule called *acetate* are produced. These are then combined with oxygen in a series of chemical reactions capable of providing enough energy-rich molecules to power every activity in our bodies. This process is called "The Krebs Cycle."

To take another example; the number of ways to make different connections between the hundred million million synapses in the human brain exceeds (is greater than) the number of atoms in the entire Universe! The nerve cell could be called the king of cells. Dr. Paul Brand says this about it: "It has an aura of wisdom and complexity about it. Spider-like, it branches out and unites the body with a computer network of dazzling sophistication. Its axons, 'wires' carrying distant messages to and from the human brain, can reach a yard in length."[14]

---

14. Yancey and Brand, *Fearfully and Wonderfully Made*, 28.

As we consider the human body, more and more wonders seem to emerge. One of the most incredible concerns the healing power of the body. If the body is pierced or wounded then, as Dr. Paul Brand explains: "an alarm seems to sound. Muscle cells contract around the damaged capillary wall, damming up the loss of precious blood. Clotting agents halt the flow at the skin's surface. Before long, scavenger cells appear to clean up debris, and fibro-blasts, the body's reweaving cells, gather around the injury site. But the most dramatic change involves the listless white cells. As if they have a sense of smell . . . nearby white cells abruptly halt their aimless wandering. Like beagles on the scent of a rabbit, they home in from all directions to the point of attack. Using their unique shape-changing qualities, they ooze between overlapping cells of capillary walls and hurry through tissue via the most direct route. When they arrive the battle begins."[15]

The white cells go on to "envelop" clusters of bacteria, like a blanket covering a body. As soon as the bacteria are absorbed, the white cells detonate a chemical explosive, destroying the invaders. Often the white cells are destroyed as well in the blast, but that doesn't matter too much. There are fifty billion active ones in the average adult human, with a backup force one hundred times as large lying in wait in the bone marrow.

Now various questions arise. How do the white cells "sense" danger, and how do they know exactly where to go to counter the danger? How do they know what measures to take in the case of different types of injury or illness? Do they have a kind of "chemical consciousness" different from our brain's self-consciousness? There are many mysteries and wonders involved in the body's amazing capacity to heal itself. Whatever might try to undermine its health, be it a cut, a bruise, an inflammation, a burn, a virus, a bunch of germs, an internal malfunction—the body reacts differently to each one. Sometimes the body cannot "cure" itself fully and needs help; but by and large doctors issue drugs or implement surgery in order that the body can continue to heal itself.

Another example of this lies in the healing of bone tissue. Bone damage is nothing like a wound or an invasion of bacteria; yet the body has its own mechanism for repairing bone fractures. Turning again to Dr. Paul Brand, he writes this about the process: "When bone breaks, an elaborate process begins. Excited repair cells invade in swarm. Within two weeks, a cartilage-like sheath called callus surrounds the region and cement-laying cells enter the jellied mass. These cells are the osteoblasts, the pothole fillers of the bone. Gradually they break down the callus and replace it with fresh bone. In two or three months the fracture site is marked by a mass of new

---

15. Ibid., 17.

bone that bulges over both sides of the broken ends like a spliced garden hose. Later, surplus material is scavenged so the final result nearly matches the original bone."[16]

Bone is a substance which is strong, yet light and efficient. It can grow continuously when necessary; it can lubricate itself, and most marvellous of all, it can repair itself when damage occurs. Even when the bone growth does not happen according to plan, and a bone graft is inserted, the body can make alternative arrangements and then attempt to heal the wound by a somewhat different method.

∽

Another wonder is that, contrary to the evidence of our senses, matter and energy have no fixed, concrete form. The elementary particles of matter are not solid or fixed. The spaces between atoms are vast compared to the atoms themselves. And then the atoms are composed of nuclei and electrons, which can be further broken down into quarks. But the electrons are in constant rapid movement and are not solid or fixed at all. As Michael Mayne has written:

> My pen is actually . . . like a flight of birds. When scientists in the nineteenth century first discovered what they called atoms, they might have preferred the metaphor of a bag of peas, for they thought atoms were indivisible, solid as snooker balls . . . It quickly became clear that there are far more fundamental things than atoms (and a thousand million million atoms could perch on a speck of dust), and that atoms are all *in motion*. They are caught up in a ceaseless chase.[17]

The particles circling the nucleus actually move at a speed of several thousand million million revolutions a second! Mayne goes on to conclude, "So my pen, my table, my balcony, my mountains are mostly holes, empty rooms enclosing the endless dance of the nuclei" (ibid). Nevertheless, even with all this space and movement, the beauty and symmetry of the things we see around us is rigorously maintained.

If we move down to the quantum (sub-atomic) world, then we find a mysterious, unpredictable realm of infinitesimal size. As light reaches an object, is it in the form of a wave or particles? At different moments it seems to change from one to the other. Not only that, but in the quantum world particles seem to appear and disappear almost at will—or randomly. No one can predict the time of their appearing or disappearing! There is, at this level

---

16. Ibid., 91.
17. Mayne, *The Sunrise of Wonder*, 113.

of reality, an Uncertainty Principle which seems to defy the scientific rules of measurement and predictability. In quantum physics there is room for freedom and randomness apparently!

༄

Now, if we look to the macroscopic dimension of life, we find that there are more stars in the galaxies of the Universe than there are grains of sand on all the beaches in the world. The distance from the Earth to our nearest star (apart from the Sun) is about twenty five million million miles. It takes about two million light years to get from our galaxy to the next—and light is travelling at the speed of 186,000 miles per second! Our galaxy, The Milky Way, contains some three hundred thousand million stars—and there are billions of galaxies in the Universe as a whole. All this is not only mind-boggling, it is literally inconceivable; beyond the capacity of minds or imaginations to grasp.

Yet a greater wonder is the fact of human consciousness: the fact that our minds can explore, examine and probe the secrets of the Universe until it is forced to surrender some of its secrets. Blaise Pascal said (in his *Pensees*) that our minds are of greater worth than the whole Universe because we alone of creatures can understand, investigate, evaluate and measure everything around us—even to the outer reaches of the cosmos.

It is strange to think that Albert Einstein was able to argue—rightly—that mass and energy are so closely interlinked that one can transform into the other. And he added that the faster an object travels, the more *time slows down* in relation to it. Thus, a clock at the equator goes a little slower than the same clock at the south or north pole. It is strange to think that two aspects of the Universe—matter and time—which we considered completely separate, are in fact closely connected together, so that the one affects the other at all times.

༄

One of the greatest wonders we see around us every day is the wonder of growth. Everything is growing all the time, unless it is inert or dead. Jesus told the parable of the seed growing secretly (Mark 4:26–29). Although this is a parable about the kingdom of God invisibly doing good in the world it is clear that Jesus saw the growth in nature as a miraculous sign in itself. "The seed would sprout and grow, he does not know how. The earth produces of itself, first the stalk, then the head, then the full grain in the head' (vv. 27–28). The marvel of the harvest comes to pass.

He tells another parable about the mustard seed; the smallest seed in the experience of his listeners, which nevertheless grows into the largest of shrubs. (Mark 4:30–32). Again, this parable is about God's kingdom, but it highlights the surprising and astonishing growth in the natural world. "When it is sown it grows up and becomes the greatest of all shrubs, and puts forth large branches, so that the birds of the air can make nests in its shade" (v. 32).

※

Now, it seems abundantly clear—even from my small number of examples—that the Universe has no lack of wonders, but it is a question of how we interpret these phenomena. Are they just serendipitous events in a random Universe, to be enjoyed and savoured, so that they enhance our appreciation of life? Or do they beg questions? Are they challenging us to understand, to reflect and to interpret them? Do they go even further than that? Are they signs of an organizing principle in life, a creative mind, a greater intelligence behind and beyond our raw experiences?

The early twentieth century Catholic writer—the author of the popular *Father Brown* stories—G. K Chesterton, was convinced that experiences of wonder should lead us to ask what they could mean. He wrote these words: "We may, by fixing our attention almost fiercely on the facts actually before us, force them to turn into adventures; force them to give up their meaning and fulfil their mysterious purpose."[18] Chesterton clearly believed that there were more superficial and deeper ways of responding to experiences of wonder and awe.

Scientific progress and the poetic imagination are linked through the valuing of this sense of wonder, for in both instances, deeper understanding and enlightenment are gained only when the discovery of something intriguing or surprising prompts us to find out more, leading us on to greater wisdom or knowledge. I would contend that scientific progress cannot be made without this initial sense of wonder at the way the world is or the way the Universe reveals itself to us. Similarly, poets cannot express deeper or more original insights unless they first have this sense of wonder at their experiences of life.

Ultimately, wonder informed by wisdom can lead on to spiritual exploration, but that is only if the person feels that an experience (of wonder) can also yield meaning and import about the nature of reality. The sense of wonder points to God, but only indirectly and only for some people. But it is for everyone to inquire inwardly what the wonders of life imply, and whether they can indeed have deeper meaning. At one extreme, the person who has lost or suppressed the sense of wonder cannot easily begin to open him or herself to the possibilities beyond raw experience. At the

---

18. Chesterton, *Tremendous Trifles*, 4.

other extreme, the person who contemplates the world and life as a place full of wonder will come to feel that the most coherent explanation for these experiences lies in acceptance of a God of wonder who reveals something of his radiance through the created order and makes sense of things, rendering our lives meaningful and the Universe intelligible.

This means, as Ruth Bancewicz argues, that "theology provides the tools to understand and interpret the experience of fascination and beauty in science."[19]

So wonder, at the deepest level, can lead to worship.

The Bible frequently speaks of "signs and wonders"—in both the Old and New Testaments. These experiences of strange power most often provoked people to ask themselves what these things could mean. They were then forced to make a choice. Is this God at work or can we find another explanation—is it my imagination? They might then forget or dismiss their experience, or explain it in a "naturalistic" way; or, alternatively, they might accept such wonders as the work of God; a revelation of his reality and his intentions with regard to the world and human beings. So even in the case of biblical wonders, the same principle applies: wonders on their own don't convince everyone to have faith. For that to happen, contemplation, reflection, wisdom and faith are all required.

4. The Reality of Good and Evil—The Moral Argument

When my wife and I were young we ran a young people's group, and one of the evening activities was something called "Moral Dilemmas." The teenagers had to consider a situation and decide which decision they would make and how they would act. They also needed to work out *why* they had taken the decision they had taken; for what reasons, on what grounds?

Here are one or two examples of the dilemmas we placed them in: "We are taught not to lie, and to speak the truth. Supposing a friend asks us whether a new coat suits her, and we really don't like it—it is ill-fitting and unflattering—do we tell the truth?"

A more serious example might be one from the Second World War: "We live in occupied France and are approached by a Jewish person to provide shelter and a hiding place in our home. We agree, but when the Nazi soldiers come to check, what do we tell them? Can it be right to lie?"

A third example is an everyday situation, but particularly relevant to a young person. "You work in a supermarket, and one day you see a friend of

---

19. Bancewicz, *God in the Lab*, 179.

yours going around the aisles. This friend apparently takes one or two things off the shelf and hides them in an overcoat. Do you report this shoplifting, or do you turn a blind eye?"

⁓

Now the question is, how do we make these moral judgements? How do we decide what is the right thing to do? Fortunately, many moral decisions are not as difficult as the ones mentioned. In those cases, different decisions could be justified by moral arguments. But that simply goes to show that different considerations might be more or less weighty. It does not prove that there is no moral law relating to good and evil. It just shows that some situations have moral arguments on both sides of the case.

Parents often hear children say, from a very young age, "It isn't fair." A little later on, they might hear two children arguing: "How would you like it if I did that to you?"

And perhaps a little later again, "You should give me back what you owe me." And then an adult might berate a stranger with "I was in the queue before you." (This last might apply more in England than elsewhere!).

Now in all these cases, the speaker is not just expressing a point of view, or an emotional dislike of certain behavior or some particular action; the speaker is rather appealing to a commonly accepted and universally understood norm of behavior. We could add to any of these complaints, "You know it is wrong!" The person accused does not reply, "I don't agree with your norm of behavior," or "I don't accept your moral code." The accused instead tries to make a special excuse or give a justification of their behavior. So the responses in each case might be, "Ah, but it's fair if you look at it differently," or "I wouldn't mind you doing that to me if you had good reason, as I do," or "I'll give you back the money as soon as I am paid," or again, "No, I think I was here before you."

These responses show that the person accused accepts the same moral code as the accuser, but is interpreting it in a slightly different way, or pointing out some reason or extenuating circumstance. That in turn seems to indicate that there is indeed a moral code to which almost everybody subscribes and which almost everybody recognizes.

⁓

If we were watching the films of *Star Wars* or *The Lord of the Rings*, we would be most unlikely to sympathize with Darth Vader or to argue that he was a good person; nor would we side with the treacherous wizard, Saruman or with the "evil eye," Sauron in *The Lord of the Rings*. Why is that? Surely because most of us easily recognize the difference between good and evil. We realize very quickly that Darth Vader (in *Star Wars*) is willing to eliminate those who oppose him, and to enslave many others to his will. In the case of Saruman and Sauron, we quickly understand that these are men who seek and love power, who want to manipulate, control and oppress other people. And they are willing to go to war—or to any lengths—to get their own way.

So this all seems to point to the fact that most people accept the reality of good and evil, right and wrong. We sense that there is a Rule of fair play or good ethical behavior. Most people would concede that being selfish, taking other people's possessions without permission, or keeping someone as a slave would all be wrong ways to behave.

Yet there have been many philosophers and others who deny that there is such a thing as a conscience, or a universal understanding of morality; who contend that there is no such thing as a common sense of the difference between right and wrong, good and evil. They would argue that these things are culturally conditioned, relating to our upbringing and to our personal preferences. They would say that different societies or civilizations have different norms, different moral codes.

Yet this is largely untrue. C.S. Lewis faced this kind of reasoning in his book, *Mere Christianity* and he investigated his critics' claims. He came to the conclusion, after much research, that in terms of general moral teaching and standards of behavior, there are in fact great similarities between different societies, civilizations and religions. Lewis writes as follows:

> There have been differences between their moralities, but these never amounted to anything like a total difference. If anyone will take the trouble to compare the moral teachings of, say, the ancient Egyptians, Babylonians, Hindus, Chinese, Greeks and Romans, what will really strike him *(sic)* will be how very like they are to each other and to our own.[20]

Lewis went to the trouble to detail his findings in another book entitled *The Abolition of Man*. He pointed up the similarities he found by putting the following case:

> Think of a country where people were admired for running away in battle, or where a man felt proud of double-crossing all the people who had been kindest to him. You might just as well try to imagine a country where two and two made five.[21]

---

20. Lewis, *Mere Christianity*, 17.
21. Lewis, *The Abolition of Man*, 17.

It is verifiably true that across cultural boundaries there are evident similarities in moral teaching. Let us take the case of what is known as "The Golden Rule." In Jesus' teaching, we find that we should do to others as we would like them to do to us. Jesus adds to this: "This is the meaning of the Law and the teaching of the Prophets" (Matt 7:12, cf Luke 6:31).

This stricture is echoed in a negative form by rabbinical Jewish teaching. The elder Hillel, who lived in the first century B.C., taught that "what is hateful to you, do not do to your fellow. This is the whole of the Law (Torah); the rest is interpretation." This negative form is also found in Ancient Egypt: "That which you hate to be done to you, do not do to another."

In Islam we find a rather similar exhortation (in the Qur'an): "Do unto all men as you would wish to have done unto you; and reject for others what you would reject for yourselves." In China, Confucius had his version of the Golden Rule (or ethic of reciprocity): "Never impose on others what you would not choose for yourself." And from Ancient India, in the Sanskrit writings known as *Mahabharata* (an epic from the seventh century B.C.) we find a wise counselor called Vidura telling King Yuddhishthira: "Treat others as you treat yourself." Vidura adds to this a list of ten teachings for good character: "listening to wise Scriptures, austerity, sacrifice, respectful faith, social welfare, forgiveness, purity of intent, compassion, truth and self-control." Most societies at most times in history would recognize the wisdom and rightness of these teachings. Or, as C.S. Lewis put it: "Human beings, all over the earth, have this curious idea that they ought to behave in a certain way, and cannot really get rid of it."[22]

⇜

St. Paul, in the first chapter of Romans, is clear that all humanity is aware of the difference between good and evil. "What can be known about God is plain to them, because God has shown it to them. Ever since the creation of the world his eternal power and divine nature, invisible though they are, have been understood and seen through the things he has made. So they are without excuse, for though they knew God, they did not honor him as God or give thanks to him, but became futile in their thinking, and their senseless minds were darkened" (Rom 1:19–21). The words he wrote or dictated have come to form the basis of what the Roman Catholic Church calls "natural theology."

Elsewhere, Paul calls this natural capacity to "know" what is right or wrong and to sense the authority of God behind it, our "conscience" (Greek *suneidesis*). This is not a word known to the Hebrew Scriptures or to Jewish

---

22. Lewis, *Mere Christianity*, 19.

rabbis. Paul takes it from the world of Greek philosophy. Paul's understanding is that while our conscience can give us a rudimentary sense of right and wrong and can be a guide for making moral choices, it is nevertheless not adequate to judge on its own. It needs to be "sharpened up" and sensitized by God's Holy Spirit working within us. The conscience has no power to overcome those appetites and desires which can lead us into trouble. The Holy Spirit provides the power and inspiration to follow the right paths and to resist evil desires.

The natural conscience can be corrupted or weakened (see 1 Cor 8:7, 10, 12 or 10:25, 27–29): it can even be "deadened." Where conscience is ignored or violated, the result can be injury to our natural humanity; to our empathy with others like us. In other words, we can become "inhuman" or "inhumane."

Paul's disciples take up the idea of conscience, and in the first letter to Timothy, we read of "a good conscience" (1:5, 19) and of a "clear conscience" (3:9 cf 2 Tim 1:3). We also read of a "seared conscience" (1 Tim 4:2) and a "corrupted conscience" (Titus 1:15).

The conscience is not the voice of God; rather it is a natural faculty bestowed upon the human consciousness to help human beings become sensitive to the moral law built into the Universe. It is linked to our sense of truth and has an objective or "real" value. In other words, it is not just a matter of opinion, even though in ethical matters there are many "gray areas" to debate and discuss. However, the discussion is carried on *in the light of* the moral law underlying the search for the good. So we can take account of many perspectives, but we should attempt to arrive at the fairest or most just decision in the light of our moral sense.

Conscience in Paul is therefore a product of the mind and heart assessing the merits of our wishes and motives, and of different situations in the world. It can be a litmus test and evaluator of our actions.

Some might regard the Moral Law not as an objective value system built into the fabric of human life, but merely as a set of social conventions; something instilled by parental guidance and general education. It may be true to say that certain values, such as good manners, consideration for others and unselfish behavior may be instilled by the interaction in family life and by parental example—perhaps also to some extent by the teaching in schools. But these things could equally well be ways of supporting and under-girding values that are in fact more objective. In other words, parents and teachers might well be responding to a sense of right and wrong which goes deeper than simply instructing a child not to speak with its mouth full, or not to snatch another child's toy, or not to scream to get its own way etc.

If we consider the moral ideals or ethical rules of various different countries, we find that on basic general principles, there is a great deal of common ground. Injunctions not to swindle another person, not to use violence (verbal or physical) to get your own way, not to sleep with a friend's wife—these and many others are ideas in common currency everywhere. This serves to give the impression that moral values are not simply locally based social conventions. On the details of how to behave, it may be that in one society there is more reverence for elderly people; in another, more rules about how and when to give hospitality or share food; in another, somewhat different rules about how children should behave in the presence of adults. Nevertheless, in most cases there is broad agreement. And if we think that one set of moral ideas is better than another, we are straight away setting up a standard, a yardstick by which to measure *the value* of ethical norms and behavior patterns. Perhaps, in the east, respect for the elderly—acknowledgement of their wisdom and life experience—might be considered "better" than the attitudes in the western world, where elderly people are often seen as burdens who require a lot of looking after, and who might be better off in a Home. Yet in that case, there are various different considerations to take into account. Is it good to take an elderly person into the family home where there are young children to look after and where both parents are working full time? What are the wishes of the elderly person? Perhaps she or he would like to remain independent of other family members. What exactly are the needs of the elderly person in question? Can they be met by an ordinary family in an ordinary home?

As we weigh these things up, we are constantly subconsciously mindful of a standard, a moral ideal, and we are balancing different considerations against the ideal to come to a final judgement which gives the best moral solution possible, even if it is a compromise. In other words, at the back of our minds, there is an objective standard against which we are measuring our decisions.

If we are sure our moral ideals are better, say, than the Nazi party's moral ideals and treatment of others, then surely there must be a yardstick against which we are comparing the two.

There are always difficult gray areas in making moral choices; and sometimes treating people with love and mercy has to be weighed up against administering justice and punishment. If someone has committed a serious crime, mercy certainly has to be tempered with justice. But the very fact that we have to make comparisons and try to find the better solution—the way which most approximates to "good morality" goes to show that we have a standard in our minds and hearts against which to measure our decisions and actions.

⁋

Now if we were to say that a dog should not have bitten somebody, or should not have barked in the night, we don't then go on to blame the dog for its poor ethical attitudes or say that the dog has behaved immorally. A dog does not have the sense of right and wrong that a human being has. All we can blame the dog for is that it did not obey our instructions, did not adhere to its training. Yet sometimes we might say that dogs do behave well. They might cooperate with one another, they might care for their young, they might show affection to their master. However, we can't say that the dog has decided that one course of moral behavior is better than another. The dog is largely acting from instinct and does what will meet its canine needs and promote harmony in its "pack"—even when that "pack" is a family of human beings! Human beings, however, do not act merely from instinct (although habits die hard!). They can have considerations which make them act in a self-sacrificial way; they can try to act lovingly when they don't feel any affection; they can put themselves out or "go the extra mile" even when it goes against the grain; they can work hard for a cause even when they are inconvenienced and made worse off financially. They can even put their lives in danger to act "rightly." As C.S. Lewis wrote:

> As for decent behavior in ourselves, I suppose it is pretty obvious that it does not mean the behavior that pays. It means things like being content with thirty shillings when we might have got three pounds, doing school work more honestly when it would have been easy to cheat, leaving a girl alone when you would like to make love to her, staying in dangerous places when you could go somewhere safer, keeping promises you would rather not keep, and telling the truth even when it makes you look a fool.[23]

⁋

So good moral behavior might well go against the grain of selfish instinct, but at the same time, it is good moral behavior that creates a safe and harmonious family, society or world at large. There can be no real happiness or peace and order in a world where criminals and fraudsters, tyrants and warlords have the upper hand. Nevertheless, the fact that family life is often dysfunctional, society is struggling to cope with criminal behavior, and the world's people are too often victims of conflict or oppression, goes to show that humanity finds it very hard—almost impossible—to live up to high

---

23. Lewis, *Mere Christianity*, 17.

moral standards; to do the right thing; to administer justice and equity for all; to love one's enemies or to live at peace with all people. Yet this does not prove that God is not active in the world or in our individual lives, just because so much has gone wrong. It only goes to show instead that human beings fail to live up to the moral standards they set themselves and which they know are right (through their conscience). The ability to choose right over wrong, good over evil is often frustrated. Sometimes moral choices are wrong because the reasoning is skewed and twisted, as in the case of a group like the so-called Islamic State or Daesh. They conceive that doing right is a matter of some imagined religious purity and this takes precedence over the sanctity of life, even in the case of innocent lives. Human nature all too often shows itself to be weak or self-interested or simply misled in its thinking.

The answer is not just to exhort people to do better or to be better. St. Paul himself realized this to his own cost: "For I do not do the good I want, but the evil I do not want is what I do. Now if I do what I do not want, it is no longer I that do it, but sin that dwells within me. So I find it to be a law that when I want to do what is good, evil lies close at hand" (Rom 7:19–21). But then Paul recognizes the Moral Law that lies within his conscience: "For I delight in the law of God in my inmost self, but I see in my members another law at war with the law of my mind . . ." (v. 23). There is an objective Moral Law, but it is frequently broken or not lived up to by frail and fallible human beings.

Thus the answer is to admit and recognize that there is indeed a clear difference between good and evil and that we are aware of this. It means that there is a mind—even a power—behind this Moral Law, assuring its authority, but that mind, that power alone has the motivating force and inspiration, the strength and authority, to help the weakened and enfeebled human will to choose the right path.

Moses confronted the children of Israel with a clear choice. It was not to obey a set of moral rules or to declare their obedience to a moral law. It was to choose to follow a path which would lead to good. That path could only be successful if the people vowed to serve God and not to rely on their own strength:

> I call heaven and earth to witness against you today that I have set before you life and death, blessings and curses. Choose life, so that you and your descendants may live, loving the Lord your God, obeying him and holding fast to him; for that means life to you and length of days, so that you may live in the land the Lord swore to give to your ancestors, to Abraham, to Isaac and to Jacob (Deut 30:19–20).

Now let us give the final word to C.S. Lewis, who was the chief advocate in modern times of the moral case for the existence of God, arguing that behind all our moral and ethical codes, decisions and norms, lies a structure in the Universe, which enables us to distinguish between right and wrong, good and evil.

> It is after you have realized that there is a real Moral Law, and a power behind the law, and that you have broken that law and put yourself in the wrong with that Power—it is after all this, and not a moment sooner, that Christianity begins to talk. When you know you are sick, you will listen to the doctor. When you have realized that our position is nearly desperate you will begin to understand what the Christians are talking about.[24]

The reality of the Moral Law and the realization of our incapacity to observe it go some way to explaining why we both hate talk of morality or of "goodness" while at the same time loving it when it affects us and our families. Someone who does good is often seen disparagingly as a "do gooder" or "holier than thou"; but if someone does us a good turn, is generous towards us and our family, or shows a loving concern towards us, we regard them with gratitude and almost turn them into a saint. If the Moral Law is seen as an impersonal obligation or duty hanging over us, we rebel. But if it has a kindly and warm personal face, then we look upon it very differently.

5. Humor—A Signal of Transcendence?

It may seem strange to alight upon *humor* as a subject for rational analysis. Can such a light-hearted—and some would say, lightweight—aspect of life give rise to serious insights into the transcendent? The answer, surprisingly, is almost certainly, yes. The sociologist Peter Berger first mooted the idea of humor as "a signal of transcendence"—albeit briefly—in his book *A Rumour of Angels* (1970). He then returned to the subject much later, writing, to my knowledge, the only full-length work on the theological implications of this subject, *Redeeming Laughter* (2014).

The essential ingredient of humor has been characterized by Peter Berger and others before him as *"incongruence"*—that is, the juxtaposing of elements which do not fit together or sit comfortably with one another. An example, in joke-form, might be when a professor, holding forth on a

---

24. Lewis, *Mere Christianity*, 37.

profound topic suddenly breaks wind. This moves the situation from the sublime to the ridiculous. Another example would be that of a politician engaged in a serious discussion who, in the middle of it, has a sneezing fit. Or again, we could point to the commonplace humor of a clown who departs from the norm by wearing over-large shoes and a big red nose. Or perhaps we could think of animals talking as if they were human characters commenting on life's foibles. One such instance would be the Alsatian who wanted to send a telegram and told the operator to write "Woof, woof, woof; woof, woof, woof." The operator, examining this "message" then told the Alsatian that for the same price he could add another "woof." "But then," replied the dog, "that would make no sense!"

Jokes often depend for their punch-line on an incongruous twist in meaning. This might be a pun with homonyms—words that sound the same, as in, "Did you hear about the man who was drowned in a bowl of muesli?" "No." "Well, he was dragged under by a strong currant!" Or the joke might depend upon a word having two different meanings: "I asked my fitness instructor, "Can you teach me to do the splits?" He replied, "How flexible are you?" I said, "Well, reasonably, but I can't make Tuesdays." Here is a third one, again relying on a word with a double meaning: "The ice cream man was found dead, covered in chocolate sauce and hundreds and thousands. The police said that he had topped himself."

Sometimes a joke simply takes us on a journey but springs a surprise— a twist—at the end, jerking us from the conventional to the absurd. This breaking out of the predictable into the unexpected follows Henri Bergson's theory (in *Le Rire* 1900) that humor is often a breaking out of mechanical modes of thought or behavior into something novel or unforeseen. Here is an example: "One day Sherlock Holmes and Dr. Watson went camping. At night they gazed at the stars. "What do you deduce from that view, Watson?" asked Holmes. "I would say that it shows that the Universe is vast, with billions of stars and galaxies. I would say there must be other planets like ours up there." Holmes then declared, "And I deduce this from it. Someone has stolen our tent!" ."

Humor is apparently good for us. A good laugh strengthens our immune system, increases our heart rate, helps us to relax and stretches many muscles in our face and upper body.

But there is more to it than that. Humor takes us out of our mundane, everyday reality—away from our routine worries and cares—and places us briefly in an alternative and more carefree world. As Peter Berger says in *Redeeming Laughter*, "The comic conjures up *a separate world,* different from the world of our ordinary reality, operating by different rules. It is also a world in which the limitations of the human condition are miraculously overcome. The experience of the comic is, finally, a promise of redemption."[25]

I have witnessed myself an occasion where three women, two of whom have difficult lives and a good many personal problems, were chatting and laughing heartily for over half an hour; then leaving smiling cheerily as if they had not a care in the world.

Humor can often help us to get through the day's minor irritations or set-backs. People with little or no sense of humor are hard to live with and heavy work in conversation. Supposing we had a few irritations in our work situation. The boss comes in and is in a bad mood; the photocopier has broken down, and the overnight cleaner has thrown out some important papers prepared for a presentation. You have to laugh or you'd cry, as the saying goes! The very accumulation of annoyances is enough to induce— not despair—laughter. This is a strange paradox.

It is also easy to laugh when one relates a mishap that seemed grim and upsetting at the time. Supposing you went out canoeing and your craft capsized. You struggled to turn the canoe upright or to escape from it, and in the process you swallowed some water and knocked your helmet over your eyes! You survived the ordeal and now, in retrospect, as you live to tell the tale, it all seems very amusing! Humor somehow magically transforms the world—but in order to engage with it, you must *disengage yourself* from the immediate; from the empirical, practical realities of normal life. The comic can restore us to a world without pain . . . Humor is often "an abstraction from the tragic dimension of human existence."[26] Someone might rejoin that black humor does in fact *highlight* the dark side of life. Yet even in that case, the humor still does alleviate the depressing reality and makes light of it.

Humor can also stop us taking ourselves too seriously. It debunks human pride and laughs at any form of deification of humanity. Humor does not tolerate the pompous and proud. The bubble of hubris has to be pricked. That is why tyrants and dictators cannot bear humor. If they are the target, humor can make them appear puffed up and foolish. Hitler hated Charlie Chaplin's film, *The Great Dictator* (1940) because he knew that he was the real butt of the satire and ridicule. His gross pretensions and megalomania were sent up in a cloud of laughter. All human pretensions to wisdom and power are thus debunked by poking fun at them.

---

25. Berger, *Redeeming Laughter*, xiv.
26. Berger, *Redeeming Laughter*, 19.

It would seem strange then to observe that the Bible apparently does not attach much importance to humor, and it is difficult to find a joke in either testament! Having said that, the printed page does not lend itself to conveying a mood or facial expression. Jesus's word about criticizing the speck of dust in someone else's eye while not noticing the plank in your own (Matt 7:3) is surely intended to be humorous, and might have been delivered with a wry smile. Also, Jesus's encounter with the Syro-Phoenician foreign woman (Mark 7:25–30) is an example of Middle-Eastern banter. The woman asks for healing for her daughter. Jesus responds by quoting his Jewish compatriots and uses the contemporary Jewish term for Gentiles—the dogs. "It isn't good to take bread from the children's mouths and throw it to the dogs!." Then she, clearly unabashed continues the repartee, saying, "Yes, but even the dogs under the table get to eat the scraps dropped by the children." Jesus evidently likes this reply a lot and assures her immediately that, thanks to her quick wit, he has already healed her daughter. This encounter—so often seen as harsh treatment—reads more like a lively joust with a good outcome. Humor is surely present here too.

In Jesus' teaching generally, simplicity and faith are regarded as superior to worldly wisdom. Jesus praises God for revealing spiritual truth, not to the self-styled wise and learned, but to the simple-hearted—the little children (Matt 11:25). This is also close to the Apostle Paul's idea that he is "a fool for Christ's sake" (1 Cor 4:10), and he elaborates on this: "For the word of the cross is folly to those who are perishing, but to we who are being saved it is the power of God" (1 Cor 1:18).

This theme of "the holy fool" is given a theological rationale a little later in the same passage: "God chose what is foolish in the world to shame the wise; God chose what is weak in the world to shame the strong" (1:27–28). There are different levels or layers of meaning in this passage (1:18–33), but the idea of "the holy fool" has had a long history in the Christian Church, and especially in Eastern Orthodox tradition. Dostoyevsky's *The Idiot* fixes on this idea for its central theme and character. The "holy fool" is an object of ridicule, but in his simplicity and humility he displays wisdom and shows up the pride and vanity of the world. A similar "holy fool" is Pierre Bezukhov in Tolstoy's *War and Peace*. In the Western Church, Francis of Assisi fits the description of the "holy fool." He "foolishly" gives away all his worldly wealth and possessions and embraces a "life of faith"—an uncertain future and the certainty of extreme poverty. Yet paradoxically he is then freed to embrace all people and all creation through his delight in simple things and his connection to the world God created.

Holy Folly can therefore be somewhat like humor in that it posits an alternative reality; a new way of looking at life. It is something of a magical transformation of life and a turning upside-down of worldly values. It is also a renouncing of worldly cares and worries. In this way, it embraces Jesus's teaching about not worrying unduly about worldly things—"what you will eat or drink, or about your body, what you will wear. Is not life more than food and the body more than clothing? Look at the birds of the air; they neither sow nor reap nor gather into barns, yet your heavenly Father feeds them" (Matt 6:25–26).

The new world which opens up to view through Jesus' teaching is the kingdom of God, which is a world where cares and worries, tears and sadness, selfish obsessions with material security are all rendered unnecessary and are laid to one side. The folly of the cross is the catching sight of this new world, which is entered through the paradox of relinquishing control and trusting Christ for our well-being and salvation. The mystery is that this unlikely world lying just beyond the immediate and practical is more real than the everyday world with its self-centered values. The rules and limitations of this-worldly reality are transcended. But instead of finding themselves in a place of impossible dreams, the likes of Francis of Assisi and other "holy fools" find themselves closer to God's heart and in a world of wonder.

So while some Christian attitudes in history have downgraded humor and seen it as shallow and facetious, the deeper religious view has been that folly—and by implication, the alternative world posited by humor—is a simpler and more joyful outlook on life.

In my own experience, contrary to the worldly view that Christians are solemn and overly serious, I have found that in Christian fellowship there is more laughter and fun than anywhere else. The normal worrying attitude to life and the taking oneself very seriously gives way in such company to the deeper reality of rejoicing in God's love and in the joy of living—in short, in the life of faith. The Danish philosopher Soren Kierkegaard once said, "Humor is the joy which has overcome the world." And the great theologian, Dietrich Bonhoeffer, who lived through the Nazi tyranny in Germany, insisted that humor sustains Christian faith through adversity—and he is one who knew this through firsthand experience.

Humor thus serves a very serious purpose in life. By pointing up the incongruities and absurdities of human experience it takes us away from a preoccupation with the seemingly all-important immediate concerns of empirical reality, pointing us to a world in which the old rules of cause and effect don't have to apply, a world of greater freedom. The American theologian Reinhold Niebuhr: "Both humor and faith are expressions of the freedom of the human spirit, of its capacity to stand outside of life, and itself, and view the whole scene . . . Laughter is our reaction to immediate incongruities and those which do not affect us essentially. Faith is the only possible response to the ultimate incongruities of existence which threaten the very meaning of our life . . . Faith is the final triumph of incongruity, the final assertion of the meaningfulness of existence."[27]

The comic is also closely related to the idea of *play*. The Catholic theologian Hugo Rahner wrote about the religious significance of play in the following terms:

> To play is to yield oneself to a kind of magic, to enact to oneself the absolutely other, to pre-empt the future, to give the lie to the inconvenient world of fact. In play, earthly realities become, of a sudden, things of the transient moment, presently left behind, then disposed of and buried in the past; the mind is prepared to accept the unimagined and incredible, to enter a world where different laws apply, to be relieved of all the weights that bear it down, to be free, kingly, unfettered and divine. Man at play is reaching out . . . for that superlative ease, in which even the body, freed from its earthly burden, moves to the effortless measures of a heavenly dance.[28]

Even if laughter as such is not often mentioned in the Bible, the word *joy (xara* in Greek) is very frequently used. In his letter to the Philippians, written from prison, Paul uses the words "joy" and "rejoice" some fifty three times. And joy is a Christian virtue even in times of adversity. Despite all his travails, Paul tells the Christians at Corinth, "We are workers with you for your joy, because you stand firm in the faith" (1 Cor 1:24). Joy is an affirmation of the blessings of redemption, and of the blessings of Christian fellowship. Paul speaks of "joy in having faith" (Phil 1:25) and also of the joy of knowing that his people are "of the same mind, having the same love, being in full accord" (2:2). Paul ends his letter with "Rejoice in the Lord always; again I will say, rejoice" (4:4).

Peter Berger tells the story of the Russian Orthodox churches which, on Easter Day, "engage in loud and prolonged laughter to celebrate the joy of the resurrection."[29] To stimulate this outburst of merriment, the preacher would often tell jokes and funny stories, occasionally with rather obscene elements! In some places, apparently, this practice has continued to the present day.

This approach perhaps echoes the mixture of faith and somewhat bawdy humor so common in the Renaissance, with Rabelais' *Gargantua* and *Pantagruel*, as well as Erasmus's *In Praise of Folly*. One of the Reformation

---

27. Niebuhr, *Discerning the signs of the times*, iii.
28. Rahner, *Man at Play*, 65.
29. Berger, *Redeeming Laughter*, 184.

divines most given to a coarse sense of humor was Martin Luther. When asked by a theological student how God occupies himself in eternity, Luther told him that God was busy cutting branches off trees to make into rods to use on people who ask silly questions! Another time, when the Archbishop of Mainz wanted to display his collection of relics, Luther told him he could add a few more; three flames from the burning bush of Moses, a piece of the flag Christ carried into hell, half a wing feather of the Archangel Gabriel and five strings of David's harp. Luther's humor might be rather sardonic—even sarcastic—for our tastes, but it does illustrate the fact that humor fulfilled an important role and function in the Church from the Middle Ages onwards.

In conclusion, the use of humor encourages people not to take themselves to seriously. It pricks their pride like a pin in a balloon and points to the truth that all people have foibles and weaknesses and can seem ridiculous at times. Human nature is fallible and this must surely be a counter to pride and self-reliance. Humor also reassures us that our daily worries and anxieties are not the be-all and end-all of our lives. Humor can take us to a place where we have a new and wider perspective on life; where we can stand aside from our everyday cares and find an oasis in the desert places of life, an island in a sea of troubles. Standing outside our mundane situation—even very briefly—can be a comfort in times of difficulty.

My grandparents had a very hard and busy life. Grandfather was a merchant seaman, often away from home; grandmother had four children to bring up, a shop to run and was secretary of a big Women's Fellowship at her church. At one time, grandfather lost all his savings by loaning his brother-in-law money to start a business. Yet, despite all the poverty and hardship, it is well known that my grandmother had a strong sense of humor and loved to make people laugh.

The very word "ecstasy" means "standing outside" or "aside" from our normal situation. The joy of humor and laughter can comfort us and sustain us through adversity and times of trouble. If this world is not a bed of roses for most people, nevertheless the pangs and setbacks of life are offset by moments of laughter and the light relief of "seeing the funny side of things."

The role of humor in life can thus be understood as enabling us to transcend the ephemeral, the temporary, the passing phases of this life; and although that does not have to be interpreted in a religious way, all the same there is something magical, or better, sacramental, about the way humor can transform life and give us the sense that in the end, all will be well and we will be free.

6. Love is at the center of Life

The old song tells us that "Love makes the world go round" and it is true to say that for most people, love is the most important thing in life. There is a French proverb which runs, "To find happiness, one thing is necessary; to love and to be loved." Without love, children can grow up to be depressed and have a low self-image. A life without love means that relationships are difficult to sustain and can easily break up. Without love, life seems to have little meaning. But with love, life looks to be more hopeful, relationships have a sweet cement to bind them, people are cared for and looked after, and everything seems to change from black and white into color.

In May 1935, the French Foreign Minister, Pierre Laval, allegedly asked Josef Stalin, the Communist dictator, to improve the situation for Roman Catholics in the USSR, so that he would not have bad relations with the Pope (Pius XI). To that request, Stalin sarcastically retorted, "And how many divisions does the Pope have?" Stalin falsely imagined that power depended upon superior force and coercion. And with regard to Christianity (and any religion) in the USSR, Stalin imagined that it could be extirpated by dint of imprisonment, persecution and closure of churches. But he was quite wrong in thinking that brute force of arms was the greatest power in the world. It is in fact love, which appears to be so weak, which is the great motivating force in people's lives. We only need to ask ourselves now how many admirers and followers Stalin has today? On the other hand, how many people are devoted to the present Pope? Or even better, how many people are dedicated to the way of Jesus Christ—the way of love for our neighbour and even for our enemies?

Sometimes love can be viewed in a rather sentimental or over-romantic light. I would guess that a majority of popular songs have the theme of love—young love, unrequited love, love thwarted, love anticipated, love at first sight, and so on. Many are based around sexual attraction and infatuation, but some have a broader theme. Sir Paul McCartney of the Beatles once said, "The world is full of people writing silly love songs." Then he added, "And what's wrong with that?"—A good point. One slightly silly love song is Louis Armstrong's "What a Wonderful World"—a song first released in 1967, which went to the top of the hit parade in many countries. The words are undeniably sentimental, and they are really about love—love of life and of the world, love of others.

> I see trees of green,
> red roses too.
> I see them bloom,

for me and you
And I think to myself
What a wonderful world.

I see skies of blue,
And clouds of white.
The bright blessed day,
the dark sacred night,
And I think to myself,
What a wonderful world.

The colors of the rainbow,
So pretty in the sky,
And also on the faces
of people going by,
I see friends shaking hands,
Saying, "How do you do?"
They're really saying,
"I love you."[30]

And so it goes on. This song struck a chord with a great many people and there is a central truth in it. It certainly seems to show that life is well worth living and that love is a wonderful fact of life. But the truth is, life is not always rosy and happy, and people do not usually go about thinking of others in terms of "I love you"—even if that might be a noble sentiment!

⁓

Jennifer Worth was the author of *Call the Midwife* and several other books about life as a midwife in the East End of London in the 1950s. During the time she worked there, she lived in St. Raymund Nonnatus House, a place which doubled up as a Convent for an Anglican religious Order, and which concerned itself with both prayer and working among the poor of the area. There were also midwives among the nuns. Jennifer Worth writes admiringly of the work of her colleagues and of the sisters: "The St. Raymund midwives worked in the slums of the London Docklands among the poorest of the poor, and for about half of the nineteenth century they were the only reliable midwives working there. They labored tirelessly through epidemics of cholera, typhoid, polio and tuberculosis. In the early twentieth century,

30. "What a Wonderful World," written by Bob Thiele and George David Weiss. Released Oct.19, 1967.

they worked through two world wars. In the 1940s, they remained in London and endured the Blitz with its intensive bombing of the docks. They delivered babies in air-raid shelters, dugouts, church crypts and underground stations. This was the tireless, selfless work to which they had pledged their lives, and they were known, respected and admired throughout the Docklands by the people who lived there. Everyone spoke of them with sincere love."[31]

Jennifer Worth writes unsentimentally and with a down-to-earth frankness about the lives of the East Enders; their trials and troubles, their daily joys and struggles. She is convinced in the books that the midwives and religious sisters were entirely motivated by love: how else could they keep going in conditions of such wretchedness; often exhausted by their work and with their lives frequently in danger? This love, shown in so many everyday tasks and deeds, at length convinced the author to search for the reason why the sisters were so devoted to their cause. She discovered Christianity and the power of the Holy Spirit in her own life and became a committed Christian in her own right. She writes at the end of *Call the Midwife* about her conversations with Sister Monica Joan in the following terms: "her constant phrase, 'Go with God,' had puzzled me a good deal. Suddenly it became clear. It was a revelation—acceptance. It filled me with joy. Accept life, the world, Spirit, God, call it what you will, and all else will follow. I had been groping for years to understand, or at least to come to terms with the meaning of life. These three small words, 'Go with God,' were for me the beginning of faith."[32]

In a fairly brief article in the *Church Times* of 4th March, 2016, Jean Vanier, founder of L'Arche ("The Ark") communities, uses the word "love" (in verb or noun form) no less than seventeen times, and he uses "compassion" or "compassionate" five times. Vanier founded his first community in 1974 to help and to house people with learning disabilities. From humble origins, there are today no fewer than a hundred and twenty four communities worldwide.

In the beginning, Jean Vanier invited two young men with serious mental handicaps to live in his house in Trosly. They did not require hospital care, but were not able to live in the community at large without support. The State could not look after them adequately, but Vanier realized that with some help these men could be integrated into society and could actually enrich the lives of others. Vanier was convinced that such people had a lot to teach the able-bodied, the successful, the people who apparently coped

31. Worth, *Call the Midwife*, 7.
32. Ibid., 319.

well with life. Yet society had become intellectualised and people too autonomous. We all needed to learn—or re-learn—the language of the heart; how to relate to others at the emotional and affective level. Vanier believed that those with mental handicaps could actually teach members of "normal society" how to love one another, how to demonstrate affection and how to enjoy life with more freedom.

In "L'Arche" communities, everybody works normal office hours, in workshops carrying out a variety of tasks, from sorting screws for factories to making pottery in craft centers; from market gardening of fruit and vegetables to the forging of metal figures and sculptures of high quality. Every community has a shop, as well as outlets to other distributors. But after work, the heart of the community is in celebration of the Eucharist and in the warmth of fellowship. The spiritual life of prayer and worship in the power of the Spirit is the engine which enables liberation and true community life.

What is remarkable is that Jean Vanier insists that those who come ready to help and to give, discover that they are helped and that they receive even more than they give. In the article, he says this: "I have been changed by the love of people with learning disabilities. This love has transformed my life, my life and my vision of salvation." He speaks with reverence of those people who have learning disabilities: "They have beautiful and sensitive hearts that are open to loving faithfully and tenderly." Of those who are the carers, Vanier says, "When they come to L'Arche, they discover that they are being invited to learn not to be a success, but to love; to create relationships of love and friendship with people who are at the bottom of the ladder of society, who are the most vulnerable and weak."

The great truth to be discovered in L'Arche communities—but also in the world outside—is that love creates bonds of friendship and wellsprings of joy that nothing else in life can create. And Vanier's conclusion is that this links people to the source of love: "L'Arche teaches us that, as we grow in goodness and compassion, even if we do not know him, we become like Jesus, who is merciful and compassionate. The source of love is in God."

༄

Now if we turn to the Apostle Paul's understanding of love, best expressed in the marvellous and ever-popular paeon of praise in 1 Corinthians 13, we there discover a rather different approach. Paul is not sentimental; he is practical. He does not pretend that life is easy and comfortable; rather it is often a difficult place to express love. However, he does certainly believe that love is "the more excellent way"—better even than possessing the gifts of the Holy Spirit such as a gift of healing, or of miracle-working. For Paul, love is about showing patience and kindness in small everyday acts; it is about disciplining ourselves to be unselfish and humble rather than self-seeking and proud. Love is about being courteous rather than rude, about being considerate rather than quick to anger. It is about blessing others rather than looking to our own benefit. Love is also linked to honesty and truth-telling: "It rejoices in the truth" (v. 6).

Ye the most interesting thing that Paul argues in this great passage is that love is the one essential virtue of our lives and that it has an eternal value. It is in fact *the* highest moral virtue: "If I speak in the tongues of mortals and of angels, but have no love, I am a noisy gong or a clanging cymbal" (v. 1). And Paul goes on to say that just three things abide; faith, hope and love. And of the three, love is the greatest. (v. 13). What does Paul mean by "abide"? Surely he is saying that these qualities are as valid in heaven as on earth. And yet there is no need for faith or hope in the world to come, because, as we come into God's presence, faith gives way to sight, and hope gives way to assurance and joyful confirmation of our hope. Only love comes to its full expression as leave this world behind: "When the complete comes, the partial will come to an end . . . Now I know only in part; then I will know fully, even as I have been fully known" (vv. 10,12). Thus, Paul is really contending that love is the most important and central quality in the whole of this life and the next. It abides despite the darkness and difficulties of this life. It abides even when we enter into the company of angels and the heavenly host.

Paul also sees love as a fruit of the Holy Spirit. In the letter to the Galatians (5:22–23) he lists the fruit of the Spirit as "love, joy, peace, patience, kindness, generosity, faithfulness, gentleness and self-control." Because Paul has "fruit" in the singular form, he almost certainly intends us to understand that love is the commanding word, since it is placed first. This means that all the other qualities are aspects of love. So love brings joy and peace into our lives and our relationships. It gradually teaches us patience, kindness and generosity. It expresses itself gently and through self-control. In addition, we can say that as Paul understands these qualities of character to be found in the Holy Spirit, then the Spirit is the source of love, and love is at the heart of God.

What Paul says is confirmed elsewhere in the New Testament. Thus John (in his first letter, 4:7–8) tells his readers that the source of human love is the love of God and therefore anyone who loves draws close to God and walks in the light: "Beloved, let us love one another, for love is from God; everyone who loves is born of God and knows God. Whoever does not love does not know God, for God is love." There are several incredible claims here: first, that the love we have in us comes initially from God; second, that the person who loves shares in the spirit of God; and third, that the one who does not love is walking in darkness rather than light.

Once I was speaking to a Frenchman about the love of God and said that John tells us that God is Love. He replied that he believed you could change the order and say that "Love is god," which was his belief. To me, this is not true, because human love is always limited and always mixed. Our moods and emotions are ever-changing, so that we cannot love in an undiluted or permanent way. Our love is rarely fixed and rarely pure. Not only that, but love has no strong motivation or encouragement for us without the deliberate outpouring of love into our hearts from God. We need this extra dose of love we gain from being open to God. How else can we love people who are unlovely, people who are nothing but trouble, people who reject us, people who are hard work for us? Yet this is what we are called to do as Christians. If we are to love even our enemies, we need God's love in our hearts. If we are to obey Paul's strictures in Romans chapter 12 without flagging or giving up, we need God's love in our hearts. This is what Paul asks of his readers:

> Let love be genuine; hate what is evil, hold fast to what is good. Love one another with mutual affection; outdo one another in showing honor . . . Bless those who persecute you; bless and do not curse them. Rejoice with those who rejoice, weep with those who weep (vv. 9, 14–15).

This whole passage is, like 1 Corinthians 13, a great hymn of praise to love.

So it is clear that for the New Testament, and for Jesus himself, love is the center and soul of life. It is the greatest power in the Universe, and it is in the heart of God himself. Yet if we pause to think a moment, we should realize that this is a very strange and wonderful fact. Why should love be so vital and so central to life if we live in a random Universe, which has no real meaning and where everything has come about in a random way?

There is something very mysterious about love. It is invisible and cannot be seen or touched. It is much more than physical attraction—or animal magnetism, as it were.

It is also more than a feeling, and in the long run has to involve choice or willpower as well as inclination. It has many forms and yet is instantly recognized as the one indivisible thing—love.

The paradox of love is that the more it is given away, the more it increases . . . And not only that, love increases greatly through suffering. Those who suffer begin to value love for their family and for the world more than anything else. And those who care for a suffering one love that person much more than when she or he was fit and well.

It seems to me that the momentous significance of love is built into the Universe because God wants it that way; he wants the Universe to share in his own being and essence. The centrality of love is a very strong argument for the existence of God; an argument which has been sadly neglected by philosophers and even theologians for a long time.

7. RELIGIOUS EXPERIENCE

Introductory

Experience is the raw material for any understanding of life. It is of course subject to analysis and rational investigation, and "explanations" of the content and significance of human experiences may vary. With regard to religious experiences this is particularly true. Some people would automatically prefer to give "naturalistic" explanations of religious phenomena—keeping "God" at arm's length; others would interpret many experiences as signs of God's activity and presence in life. However, for most of those who have undergone a converting experience, or even have had a strong sense of God's presence and reality, a purely "naturalistic" explanation just will not do.

In a very significant study entitled *The Idea of the Holy* (1923), Rudolf Otto enquired into the religious element in human experience, coining various splendid expressions for this, such as "the numinous," "the supra-rational," "the wholly other" and, most mesmerizing of all, the "mysterium tremendum et fascinans." Otto's aim was to show that religious experience is not irrational, but is rather "non-rational" or "supra-rational." He argued that if rational argument is not firmly based on real experience, then it becomes pure theorizing. In the case of religious experience, it is speculating about God without any direct apprehension of God. Rationalism at worst turns what he calls "the Holy" into an ethical ideal instead of a sense of God's presence. This has led to confusion about what "holiness" is ever since. Is it living up to high moral ideals, or is it an inner purity and the glory of God within us?

Otto also considered that the Early Church's attempt to understand its own experience of God led to the formulation of doctrine and dogma, and especially that of the Trinity. The danger then is that formulations of doctrine become normative for the religious life instead of experience of God and a sense of God's presence.

Breaking down the experience of "the numinous," Otto argued that a person in the presence of something beyond everyday life would feel a sense of dependence or contingency—in short, feel small and humble. On the other hand, there would be a sense of an overpowering or awesome manifestation. This would result in a holy fear and a desire to prostrate oneself. That experience is hard to explain in words, but is supremely significant for the person involved in it.

If we turn to another classic book; William James' *The Varieties of Religious Experience* (1902), we find both an analysis of different types of experience, but also firsthand accounts of encounters with "the numinous" or "the divine." James writes about religious experience from an agnostic, but sympathetic standpoint. He is also keen to interpret his material from a psychological and scientific point of view.

James distinguishes "healthy-minded religion" from that of "the sick soul." The former approaches any religious experience from a balanced, sane and stable faith; the latter tends towards the neurotic and fanatical.

James recognizes that in many cases intense religious experience serves to integrate and unify the personality. He is convinced that any such experience should therefore be judged by its fruits. If it leads to useful action and purposeful living, and shifts the emotional center towards love and "harmonious affections,"[33] this is evidence of good fruits. And in the longer run it should lead to greater freedom, simplicity of life, strength of soul, purity and passion. This all derives from what James calls an ongoing "sense of the presence of a higher and friendly power."[34]

James' investigation then moves on to an examination of saintliness and mysticism. He regards true mysticism not as a "passive quietism," but as the wellspring of action. So religious experience—the consciousness of a higher power—can in the long term result in a saintliness which brings peace of mind and charitable behavior:

> There is veritably a single fundamental and identical spirit of piety and charity common to those who have received grace; an inner state which before all things is one of love and humility, of infinite confidence in God, and of severity for one's self, accompanied by tenderness for others.[35]

Interestingly, James sees the motivating power of religious experience as something common to all major faiths, and common to very different

---

33. James, *The Varieties of Religious Experience*, 279.
34. Ibid., 274.
35. Ibid., 260.

branches of Christianity too. He quotes approvingly the French writer, Sainte-Beuve: "The fruits peculiar to this condition of the soul have the same savour in all, under distant suns and in different surroundings, in St. Teresa of Avila just as in any Moravian brother of Herrnhut."[36]

James contends that there is no one *religious* experience or emotion; in fact, "nothing whatever of a psychologically specific nature."[37] What distinguishes *religious* experience as such is the object towards which it is directed, or better, to which it responds. The *religious* experience is also characterized by something "solemn, serious and tender."[38] This is not quite the fear and awe of Otto's *mysterium tremendum,* but is linked to "a sense of reality, a feeling of objective presence"; in other words, to a sane and rational but extraordinary experience.

Religious experience is thus the fundamental raw material of our apprehension, just as much as is any sensory experience of life. It is not easily subjected to testing or "proving," but is eminently susceptible to reasoned analysis. It is similar to what Henri Bergson called "intuition," as James himself admits[39] when he says; "If you have intuitions at all, they come from a deeper level of one's nature than the loquacious level which rationalism inhabits."[40]

A religious experience can be a heightened awareness of something as straightforward as the harmony and beauty of nature. The poet Walt Whitman is cited by James as one who often reacted to the world with a quasi-religious emotion. He quotes Whitman's biographer, Dr. Bucke: "All natural objects seemed to have a charm for him. All sights and sounds seemed to please him."[41] James then adds: "The only sentiments he allowed himself to express were of the expansive order . . . so that a passionate and mystic ontological emotion suffuses his words, and ends by persuading the reader that men and women, life and death, and all things, are divinely good."[42] Whitman was not a conventionally "religious" poet, but James is convinced that he is a "restorer of the eternal natural religion."[43]

If we move on to more obviously religious experiences, then conversion provides many and varied examples of the type. James quotes a whole variety of case studies: from Luther's move from an obsession with his sin finally

36. Ibid.
37. Ibid., 27.
38. Ibid., 38.
39. Ibid., 73.
40. Ibid., 70.
41. Ibid., 84.
42. Ibid., 85.
43. Ibid.

issuing in an experience of grace and liberation, to a certain Colonel Gardiner, an Oxford graduate, who had an experience when he was, on his own confession, in perfect health and in no way troubled about his soul. In fact, on the day of his conversion, he was not even thinking about God. Yet, while he was reading quietly, he had an overwhelming experience, and later wrote; "God met me face to face and I shall never forget the meeting." He had a powerful feeling "that there was another being in my bedroom, though not seen by me. The stillness was very marvellous and I felt supremely happy. It was unquestionably shown me, in one second of time, that I had never touched the Eternal, and that if I died then, I would most inevitably be lost. I was undone. I knew it as well as I now know that I am saved. The Spirit of God showed it me in ineffable love; there was no terror in it; I felt God's love . . . powerfully upon me. All the time, I was supremely happy; I felt like a little child before his father."[44]

Two famous conversion stories

Now, to take a biblical example, the conversion of St. Paul on the road to Damascus is so well known that the phrase "a Damascus experience" is used in common conversation. Paul's conversion is in fact one of the pivotal events of the entire New Testament. It is described in detail no less than three times by Luke in *The Acts of the Apostles* (Acts 9:1–28; 22:1–21 and 26:4–23). Paul himself also refers or alludes to his own conversion a number of times, but without giving much circumstantial detail (1 Cor 9:1; 15:8–10; Gal 1:13–17; Phil 3:4–11). In 2 Corinthians 4:6, Paul speaks in a way which sounds reminiscent of his encounter with the risen Jesus Christ: in a memorable phrase he writes of "the light of the glory of God in the face of Jesus Christ." If this is indeed an allusion to his conversion, then it shows how he understood his experience as being an encounter with a divine being—the Lord. No longer could he think of Jesus as being a messianic impostor, stirring up heresy and malpractice among his followers; leading them astray by placing his words above the Law of God (Torah). From now on, Paul would not see Jesus merely "from a human point of view" (2 Cor 5:16), or continue to persecute his disciples. Now he had come to accept that Jesus was in fact the Son of God.

So what actually happened at the time of Paul's conversion? The details in Luke's accounts vary slightly, but the words addressed to Paul are consistent: "Saul, why are you persecuting me?" Paul then asks, "Who are you,

---

44. Ibid., 221–22.

Lord?" The reply comes, "I am Jesus whom you are persecuting." It is clear that Paul is surprised by this sudden vision or manifestation, and believes that he has been confronted by a heavenly being, whom he must address as "Lord." Jesus' question is intensely personal. He does not ask, "Why are you persecuting my church (or 'my people')?" Rather he asks "Why are you persecuting *me*?" This heralds a new and close personal relationship with Paul, who is then commissioned. He must go to the Gentiles "to open their eyes, so that they may turn from darkness to light." From that time on, Paul sees himself as *the* apostle to the Gentiles.

So this encounter is three things in one: a personal call, a converting experience (which turns Paul's life upside down), and a commissioning to a new and vital role in the life of the early Church. Paul later has to justify his apostolic authority, and he always refers back to his meeting with the risen Christ: "Have I not seen Jesus our Lord?" (1 Cor 9:1); or he asserts that he is "a servant of Jesus Christ, called to be an apostle, set apart for the glory of God" (Rom 1:1). In another place, Paul speaks of "seeing the glory of our Lord Jesus Christ with unveiled faces" (2 Cor 3:18). This could well be a reference to his life-changing experience. And in 1 Corinthians 15:8, where Paul relates the resurrection appearances of Jesus Christ, he ends his list with, "And last of all, as to one aborted, he was seen by me too." Paul puts his encounter on a par with those of the twelve disciples.

Because of his experience, Paul's whole perspective on life is changed. He now comes to regard Jesus not only as the Jewish Messiah, but as the Saviour of the World and as the divine agent of God, who has inaugurated a new age for humanity; he has ushered in the age of the Holy Spirit to replace the age of the Law. Having had an exemplary career as a Pharisee, Paul now becomes the most enthusiastic and devoted of Christians, being willing to suffer all manner of hardship, abuse and punishment for the sake of his Lord (see 2 Cor 11:22–30). The only thing that matters now for Paul is "to gain Christ, and to be found in him" (Phil 3:8–9). He even dismisses all his past life as so much dross—*skubala* in Greek; literally "dung."

Paul's experience was not solicited or sought after. It came as a shock to him; and yet it deeply affected the rest of his life. It was a revelation to him, that he never once doubted: "The gospel proclaimed by me is not of human origin; for I did not receive it from a human source, nor was I taught it, but I received it through a revelation of Jesus Christ" (Gal 1:11–12). The experience not only revealed to Paul who Jesus really was (or is), but also revealed to him the purpose of his whole life.

Thus from the time of this experience, Jesus became the focal point of Paul's life and belief system. From then on he regards his life as "gaining Christ and being found in him" (Phil 3:8–9). Faith in Christ becomes the cornerstone of his theology, and his relationship with the risen Christ the motivating force of his endeavours.

It is difficult, if not impossible, therefore, to deny that Paul had an overwhelmingly powerful and meaningful encounter with Jesus Christ. It affects everything Paul thinks and does from that time onwards. His whole theology develops out of this experience, and however we interpret it, we cannot deny the reality of it.

If we now turn to John Wesley's conversion experience, it seems much more low-key and muted. Yet, in a similar way to Paul's, it affected the entire subsequent life and work of Wesley in a thoroughgoing way. Wesley underwent this experience on May 24th, 1738. Yet this was *after* he had attended the Holy Club at Oxford University, had studied for ordination and become a curate in the Church of England, then had become a missionary in Georgia, USA. All through that time he adhered to a legalistic and formal kind of Christianity. As a missionary, his rigid, rather autocratic approach made him unpopular, both with settlers and with native Americans. So, on his return home, he was depressed and self-critical, very much wanting a fresh start in his Christian life. On the day of his conversion, he opened his New Testament at five in the morning and read some words from 2 Peter 1:4, "[God] has given us . . . his precious and very great promises, so that you may escape from the corruption that is in the world . . . and may become participants in the divine nature." This verse played on Wesley's mind, and in the afternoon, he attended a service at St. Paul's and heard the anthem, "Out of the deep have I called unto Thee, O Lord: Lord, hear my voice." In the evening he went reluctantly to a meeting in Aldersgate Street, where someone was reading Luther's preface to the letter to the Romans—not a very promising start, we might think. Yet Wesley later that night wrote in his Journal these words:

> About a quarter before nine, while he was describing the change which God works in the heart through faith in Christ, I felt my heart strangely warmed. I felt I did trust in Christ, Christ alone for salvation. And an assurance was given me, that he had taken away *my* sins, even *mine*, and saved me from the law of sin and death.[45]

Wesley's rather understated description of the "heart strangely warmed" did not mean that this was a passing occurrence. It changed his whole life for good, and he became a more passionate and convinced believer, with a great

45. Wesley, *Journal*. 24.05.1738.

love for God and a heart for ordinary people. No longer the rigid, remote academic, he was from then a man transformed.

But was this merely the resolution of a psychological crisis? If so, it nevertheless bestowed upon Wesley a continuing sense of God's close presence, which lasted the rest of his life. His experience could be likened to the kindling of an unquenchable fire in the bones. His preaching changed utterly. He now had a powerful and marked effect upon others. Sometimes the congregation would listen quietly, then break into noisy raptures at the end... For example, on 18th September, 1748, at St. Stephen's Down in Cornwall, Wesley comment in his Journal: "The moment I had done, the chain fell off their tongues. I was really surprised. Surely there was never such a cackling made on the banks of the Cayster or the Common of Sedgemoor." By contrast, on 12th December, 1742, at Newcastle, the people "stirred neither hand nor foot." And when the sermon was over, "a great and solemn silence descended, and everyone went away from the place pensively." But again, at other times, there was great emotion and commotion. At Everton, in 1759, "those under conviction of sin would fall to the ground, convulsed with sighs and sobs, or cry out in the agony of their souls. Wesley would call on the rest to bow in prayer whilst he pleaded for the release of the captives."[46]

Whatever form the manifestations at Wesley's meetings happened to take, one thing is for sure: these were not passing phases. Many of the people convicted by his preaching were soundly converted, and then formed into "societies," which later became Methodist churches.

If a religious experience or a conversion experience is to be judged by its long-term fruits, then Wesley's own and those of his converts could give testimony to a permanent change in their lives, wrought by their initial experience. This change was not only a new direction in their lives and a new faith in God; it was also a life dedicated to love for neighbour, a new moral earnestness and a new desire to please God. Wesley did not allow his converts to feel that through conversion they had been "saved" and that nothing further remained to do. He taught that conversion was the beginning, and salvation itself was a matter of persevering in the Christian life, making progress, striving after saintliness—also called "scriptural holiness" or "perfect love." There was a dynamic to the Wesleyan teaching and way of life, which found expression in the weekly class meeting, where members would study the Bible, but also report on their "walk with God" and on their progress in the Christian life. The assumption behind this theology was that after conversion one's whole life should be lived in the presence of God, and in the experience of God's love and mercy—in short, in holiness

---

46. Skevington, *The Burning Heart*, 164.

of life. Thus, for Wesley, conversion was only the start of a new and ongoing relationship with God and with the risen Lord.

Contemporary experiences

Now, both of our examples of religious experiences so far are conversion experiences (of St. Paul and of John Wesley). And both are from a good while ago in time. Religious experiences are of course up to date as well as historic, and they take many forms. This being the case, I will relate a few contemporary examples known to me.

Professor Janet Martin Soskice, chair of the divinity faculty at Cambridge University (U.K.), tells in the Church Times of 4th March, 2016 of how, at the age of twenty, she had an experience of God, even though her parents were not Christians, and she had no connections with the Church. It came "quite out of the blue," and Professor Soskice describes it as though she "had fallen secretly in love, which perhaps I had." She became aware "that the world was profoundly ordered to the Good." In other words, her experience of God was mediated through an experience of the harmony and moral order—the rationality—of the world around her. But this experience also felt like falling in love!

Since that time, Professor Soskice has become a world-renowned theologian and academic, but what does she now say of her faith? She writes in the same article: "Faith is now richer, deeper, steadier than the dizzy days of falling in love with God, but much the same in substance." Her daily walk with God is not like an "emotional high" or a state of constant excitement—of course not—but it is firm and stable. She adds, finally; "I believe that the Christian God speaks to us in many ways: through Scripture, preaching, friends, political crises." The experience of God is often indirect, but is none the less real.

My second example concerns a Youth Group leader called Brian in my church when I was younger. He told me the story of his conversion and in fact it was a somewhat similar experience to Janet Soskice's. He was sitting in a lecture hall, slightly bored and distracted, when suddenly the whole place seemed to become suffused with light, and he had an experience of everything coming together in harmony and order, everything becoming interlinked, held together in a spiritual unity which he interpreted as the work of the Spirit of God. Everything made a coherent and rational whole, and for Brian the world suddenly made sense and he himself fitted into the pattern of things. Brian became a Christian and has been so for the all of his life ever since.

My third example shows how sometimes events seem to "work together" in a series of "coincidences" (or what some might call "God-incidences"). When my wife Jane was young, before I knew her, she went away to study. At the age of eighteen and in her first year at College, she was an agnostic, living in an environment of freedom and independence, but searching for direction in life. She heard that her grandmother was ill and had been taken into hospital. Jane was close to her grandmother, since she had shared a bedroom with her every time the grandmother came on one of her extended visits. So Jane went home and heard that her grandmother was making a recovery. However, when she came away from the hospital visit, she had a strange premonition that she would never see her grandmother again.

She went back to continue her studies, and, a short while later, she had an unexpected phone call from her mother telling her that her grandmother had died. Jane's mother seemed shaken and disturbed, and so Jane prepared to go home again in order to attend the funeral and to try to comfort her distraught mother. On the train, she sat in a small compartment with three older ladies. Everyone was friendly and they started talking. Jane explained about her grandmother and how she wanted to help her mother. To her surprise each of the three women had a story of how their Christian faith had helped them through a difficult time in life. They all had words of encouragement and wisdom. Later, Jane saw this as the first step in her own journey of faith. She was given the strength to help to console her mother and had a glimmer of hope and faith for herself.

The most distressing part of the funeral for her was when the coffin was lowered into the grave and earth was scattered on top of it. It seemed very final, as though life had come to a very definite full stop. She remembered little of the funeral service, except that the twenty third Psalm was read. She went to bed that night feeling sad and empty, preoccupied with the image of earth thudding into the coffin lid—earth to earth, dust to dust, ashes to ashes. She wondered to herself whether there could possibly be more to life than a short span with a meaningless finale. So she prayed, "If there is a God, will you please show me." She took a small Bible off the bedroom shelf—a Bible she had been given at her baptism, and had never read—and, not knowing where to look for comfort, opened it at random. This is, by the way, not a method she would normally recommend to anyone now! However, the Bible lay open at the twenty third Psalm again. She felt comforted and had a sense of warmth enfolding her. This was the beginning of her search for faith—it sowed the seed. On reflection, she thought finding the Psalm could just be coincidence, but on the other hand, she felt it was indeed a sign from God. She found herself able to sleep peacefully at last.

Since that time, on occasions when Jane has felt troubled or dismayed, the twenty third Psalm has often made an appearance—more often than coincidence ought to allow. Apart from that, Jane explored Christianity in a more rational way, and her nascent faith came alive, giving her hope and purpose in life. Jane was not deliberately searching for a religious experience for herself. Her reason for going home was to help and bless her mother in a time of distress. But through her good motives, God showed his presence through a few people and through a few simple signs, to encourage her. Sometimes when our intentions are good, we link ourselves to God's purposes and to his will and he is able to reveal himself in the unfolding events of life. This seems especially true in a time of trouble, when we are more reflective. For it is in giving that we receive. Jane has been a convinced and faithful Christian ever since.

My final contemporary example concerns someone well known to me, called Jason. He had a very serious car accident on 16th October, 2004. He was waiting at a busy junction before crossing a major road. In the passenger seat he had a friend he was taking home, before returning to his own house. The lights changed to green and Jason proceeded in first gear. As he pulled out, a Vauxhall Calibra, which had jumped the red lights, accelerated straight into the side of Jason's car, crumpling the driving seat to half its normal width, and hitting Jason with such force that he was shunted into his friend, breaking three of the friend's ribs and moving his own internal organs violently to the left side of his body.

The two young men in the other car were panicked, and ran away from the scene, pursued by a few members of the public, including RAF officers. They were only apprehended much later. It was discovered that their car was not insured and the driver only possessed a provisional licence.

Jason's friend was not too badly hurt, but the roof of Jason's car had to be cut off in order to lift him out to safety and into the ambulance. Some time later, when he woke up in hospital, his first thoughts were, and I quote, that "things were so grave they were threatening my existence." He was put into intensive care in a special tilting bed to help his organs to resettle. On two separate occasions, Jason's German wife, who was then six months' pregnant, was told that the following twenty four hours would be critical.

Then Jason entered a dream-like, comatose world of dark thoughts, phantasms and nightmares. He was in the dark forest of his own tormented psyche. In this state, he had several delusions. First, he was convinced that his friend had separated from his wife; then that his eldest son had been arrested; then that he was stuck in an office with a midwife; then finally that one of the nurses caring for him was an infiltrator intent on killing him! In his normal self, Jason is a cheerful and positive person; so he found this mood of hopelessness and troubled imaginings very distressing. He was also in a lot of pain and discomfort.

Meanwhile, Jason's wife, who had been brought up by a Catholic mother and Protestant father, and who had gone to church as a young girl with her grandmother, had, at a youthful age, become disillusioned with Christianity, and had lost her faith completely when a close friend of hers was killed in an earthquake in Turkey. Nevertheless, after all these fallow years, she now turned to prayer as a last resort, while Jason lay prostrate in his hospital bed.

Jason was in intensive care for two months, with two nurses caring for him twenty four hours a day. He was in a state of depression—even despair—when, out of the blue, one day he felt himself being lifted out of his bed and taken ever upwards—supported at both ends by firm and strong hands. Whoever was lifting him did so effortlessly, with immense strength. He felt very safe. Higher and higher he went, above the fog of misery and gloom he had been lying in. His pain gradually disappeared and he felt perfectly well. The darkness was replaced by a dazzling whiteness, with the background of a wonderful orange sunset, extending into the far distance, to the very curve of the Earth's horizon. Jason felt happy and relieved; he had no fear. Then he heard a voice say to him, "This is how powerful I am. Stay with me." Jason wondered what this meant and thought about how he could gauge that power. But it was all-encompassing. He could not see anyone, but he had the sense that he was being bathed in light. All the dark physicality of his earlier experiences had evaporated. From a bleak and hopeless place, he had been lifted into a joyful and positive place. He was sure that it was God who was helping him and showing him something. But he had had no dealings with God before. He had not been raised in a Christian home, had no knowledge of Scripture and had no particular interest in religion. As he told me, "It was just not on my radar."

Yet out of his experience, Jason felt that God wanted him to find a new path in life and to learn through the study of the Bible. "I knew I had to do something," he thought. He felt he had to change and make new commitments.

When he came out of hospital, he discovered that two of his work colleagues were Christians. One liked to help him in his newfound faith with little encouragements; "he was drip-feeding me daily." The other Jason saw less frequently, but when he did see him, this new friend always made an impact. Once, he gave Jason Mark's gospel to read, another time he explained the reason Jesus came to Earth, another time he advised Jason to go to a church and talk to the vicar about his experiences. Both friends felt that Jason would benefit by being among Christians. So he gradually started to learn about his new faith, made new friends and read the Bible... He has been involved with church ever since, and in 2015, in a packed church and a joyful service, with some three hundred and fifty people, he and fourteen others were confirmed.

Since his accident, Jason has not had an easy time. He has required further treatment and surgery. Recently, he had a big operation on an incisional hernia. During this intervention, a few verses of Matthew's gospel came to him (Matt 6:25–27): "Do not worry about your life, what you will eat and what you will drink... Look at the birds of the air; they neither reap nor sow, nor gather into barns and yet your heavenly Father feeds them." A little later on, he heard a sermon on God being described as "powerful." This reminded him of his own experience in hospital. By contrast, he had also learnt that Jesus' coming meant that God laid aside his power and glory to enter human life and to show the human race what God was like in human terms and how much he loved us all.

Jason's experience was unique, but it was nothing like the dark fantasies he had before—perhaps due to the large doses of morphine. It was through an intense experience of suffering that he came to know God. His experience was more like the cleansing of his soul, a foretaste of heaven and a new sense of God's love and mercy reaching down to him to offer him a new life. However we might choose to interpret his experiences, the results in his life have been ongoing and long-lasting. He still has the sense that God is with him, and, as promised, will always be with him, through life and death.

∽

There are many and varied examples of religious experience, as is evident from these short accounts, and they can come from different faith traditions. I have focused particularly on those relating to Christian faith, as this is more familiar to me, and because a good part of this book draws on the biblical responses to life's experiences.

∽

Concluding words—in conversation with David Bentley Hart

A work recently published by an American philosopher and theologian of the Eastern Orthodox tradition, David Bentley Hart, is entitled *The Experience of God: Being, Consciousness, Bliss* (2013). Bentley Hart takes issue with the "new atheists" of our own times over their understanding of God. The "God" attacked by these atheists, he argues, is a kind of "cosmic craftsman"—a "demiurge"—who created the Universe (rather badly) out of materials separate from himself, and then he contrived to set in motion all the processes needed to create galaxies, stars, and planets; then life forms, including plants and trees, birds and animals and human beings. This "demiurge" started up the whole business of the Universe with a "Big Bang" or something similar. This "God," Bentley Hart contends, is external to the Universe; that is, absolutely transcendent, and is not necessary to that Universe once it has started up, because it can continue by itself, like a gigantic machine which has an "intelligent design." By the way, this is not the same as building into the Universe the blueprints for the emergence of all the materials and life forms which have come about. Such a Universe is not like a machine, but more like an organism. Now if the processes in the Universe of the "demiurge" can be explained in a naturalistic way, (for instance, using evolutionary theory), without reference to an external agency—then in that case, we can dispense with the idea of a God (or "demiurge") altogether (except that some might argue that a god is needed to fill in the "gaps" in our knowledge. This case only holds while such "gaps" persist.).

The Christian God is not like this at all, says Bentley Hart. He is not one very powerful being among other beings. Rather, he is the *cause and source of all being*. The Christian God is different in kind to all things which exist contingently. He is the light of Being itself: "To speak of God properly is to speak of the one infinite, omnipresent, uncreated, uncaused, perfectly transcendent of all things, and for that reason absolutely immanent to all things."[47]

The true God is accessible to humans through their experience of life, because the Universe itself is "open." In atheism, it is a closed, materialistic system. But for Bentley Hart, everything that is contingent lies open to the upholding and creative power and activity of God at every moment. This means that God is involved in all aspects of life at all times—not just at some hypothetical moment of creation.

Bentley Hart uses the terms "Being, Consciousness and Bliss" as terms which designate God's nature, but which also give "a phenomenological explanation of the human encounter with God."[48] In defining God's nature in this threefold manner, he is using a Hindu term for the godhead, which has sometimes been adopted as a symbol of the three persons of the Christian Trinity. He elucidates this use as follows:

---

47. Bentley Hart, *Atheist Delusions*, 30.
48. Ibid., 44.

They perfectly designate those regions of human experience that cannot really be accounted for within the framework of philosophical naturalism without considerable contortions of reasoning and valiant revisions of common sense. They name essential and perennial mysteries that, no matter how we may try to reduce them to purely natural phenomena, resolutely resist our efforts to do so, and continue to point beyond themselves to what is "more than nature."[49]

Elsewhere, Bentley Hart argues that the empirical sciences yield knowledge of physical processes, but are not suitable to analyze "other dimensions of reality"—"starting with the most fundamental dimension of all—existence as such—that constitute our knowledge of, judgements about, and orientations toward the world."[50] The example is then given of the physical processes that take place in the brain to give rise to experiences, and particularly, religious experiences. Bentley Hart insists that although "there are certainly neurological activities attendant upon religious or mystical experiences—how could there not be?—but in no way does that imply that such experiences are *nothing but* neurological activities. Certain brain events attend the experience of seeing a butterfly or of hearing a violin as well, but that ought not to lead us to conclude that butterflies and violins are only psychological fictions."[51] Bentley Hart is in effect saying that "religious" experiences should be judged by the same criteria as any other experience of the external world.

This is all well put, and it is certainly true to say that many atheists, and even some neuroscientists, appear to want to reduce thoughts, memories and experiences to a collection of chemicals in the brain, as if they are reducible to material manifestations alone. This not only eliminates the common sense notion that we have *a mind* as well as a brain, but it makes very problematic the question of how we apprehend the external world at all.

All of the preceding can relate to general experience of life, but what of specifically "religious" experiences? Bentley Hart characterizes these by saying that they are not different *in kind* from any other experiences. Rather, with regard to "religious" experiences, "one is seeking an ever deeper communion with a reality that at once exceeds and underlies all other experiences."[52] Religious experiences are not just unusual experiences alongside other, more commonplace, experiences. They are experiences

49. Ibid.
50. Ibid., 318.
51. Ibid., 319.
52. Ibid., 320.

which go deeper into the nature of reality, the essence of life, the fundamental make-up of the Universe.

Bentley Hart regards contemplation, and especially contemplative prayer, as leading to this deeper apprehension of life's mysteries. For him, it is an "extremely simple thing. It often consists in little more than cultivating certain habits of thought, certain ways of seeing reality, certain acts of openness to a grace that one cannot presume, but that has already been granted . . . It is before all else the practice of allowing the existential wonder that usually comes to us only in evanescent instants to become instead a constant inclination of the mind and will, a stable condition of the soul, rather than a passing mood."[53]

Mysticism would, on this analysis, be a more advanced stage of contemplation, requiring one to enter into the depths of the self, into one's own "heart," to seek nothing less than union with God in love and knowledge. In this section I have deliberately avoided engaging with mysticism. There are many and varied writings by mystics and on the subject of mysticism, which can easily be consulted. I have preferred, instead, to dwell upon everyday and ordinary human experience, which can often include experience of God or of heightened states of awareness. The strict disciplines and phases of purgation and illumination in mystical experience are not really the proper subject of a book on the human condition and on general human experience. However, it is worth saying that mystical experience, by and large, is not the product of a fevered imagination, and hardly ever has the character of strange visions and hallucinations. Its "events" are more commonly rationally described and are open to rational study. They frequently result in healthy and joyful outcomes.

Twenty first century society has concentrated upon technological approaches to life, which excel in the manipulation of the material world: medicines, mass communications, computer creativity, scientific research through experimentation; and lately the development of "virtual reality" and life-like role-play games. All of these belong largely to the same material order of reality. The realm of the spiritual—so often expressed through the medium of great art, literature, philosophy, theology and real-life experience—that realm is sadly neglected and sometimes even denigrated or dismissed. It is all too easy today to assume that a mechanical theory of reality is the whole and complete picture of reality. In modern life, the silent depths of being can effortlessly be lost among superficial distractions, the noise of the mass media, an obsession with shopping and spending, and

---

53. Ibid., 322.

what Bentley Hart beautifully sums up as "a ceaseless storm of artificial sensations and appetites."[54]

Bentley Hart's book ends with the rather Platonic observation that "the mere possession of information is not yet knowledge, and that knowledge is not yet wisdom, and. therefore whatever one thinks one understands might in fact be only the shadow of some greater truth."[55] His investigation into *The Experience of God* is in truth a rather abstract, philosophical work. It is certainly penetrating and forceful in its unmasking of the weaknesses of the atheist position, but his positive case might have been strengthened and made even more convincing with a larger number of examples of experiences from real life. And while "Being, Consciousness and Bliss" serve to characterize the nature of God at a philosophical level, it is arguable that, from the perspective of ordinary experience of life, a better triad might be suggested; Being, Creativity and Love.

"Being" is a difficult concept, and a better term might be "Reality" or "Intelligence." The second word, "Creativity" yields the idea that God is essentially the creator of all things—not only in the beginning, but in a continuing and continuous process of engagement with the Universe. Thirdly, "Love" is central to God's nature, as we have seen, and it encompasses "bliss" and other characteristics such as "generosity," "self-giving," "longing," "friendship" and the "making of relationships" in the highest sense.

If God is indeed "Being, Creativity, Love," and we humans are made in God's image, then we too have a nature that is open to hidden depths of reality in our inner being and also in our outward apprehension.

We have an inner life—a sense of *being*—which is profound and mysterious—not only in terms of thoughts and memory, but also in terms of the subconscious mind. We can live in the past (through memories) and the present (through attention to life in the here and now), but also imagine and conceive the future (through imaginative ideas). This allows us to make plans, dream up possibilities and organize our lives. Our capacity to analyze, ponder and reflect means that our being—our essential self—is in touch with the depths of Being in the world beyond us.

We too are *creative* and are fulfilled through the creativity of work, craftsmanship, making and repairing, writing and self-expression, engineering, artistic endeavour, helping others, being useful, learning new skills, parenting, healing, making things anew. There are many ways of being creative, and they help us to find ourselves, to reach our potential and become who we should be.

54. Ibid., 329.
55. Ibid., 330.

We too are *made for love*, and should be willing to give ourselves in love to others; caring for and making sacrifices for those in need; being a blessing and bringing comfort and joy; acting as peacemakers and people of goodwill; creating warm relationships and contributing towards happy and healthy communities. In expressing our true nature of Being, Creativity and Love, we not only find purpose and fulfilment in our own lives, but we simultaneously draw closer to God and come to experience God in everyday situations and activities.

SECTION TWO

A SUFFERING WORLD—
BIBLICAL RESPONSES

CHAPTER THREE

THE DEBATE IN THE OLD TESTAMENT

Now I AM GOING to turn to the Old Testament and look at reactions and responses to suffering in the books of the Hebrew Scriptures.

A great deal of the Old Testament depicts situations of great suffering. There is the slavery and harsh treatment endured by the Hebrews in Egypt; then their suffering in the Sinai desert after escape from the Pharaohs. There are the cries of lament and distress in many Psalms; there is the disillusionment and near despair of the Book of Ecclesiastes. Then the whole book of Lamentations is a long cry of desolation emanating from the terrible suffering caused by the siege and eventual sacking of Jerusalem and the subsequent widespread slaughter and the taking of people into exile.

Next, there is the suffering of the prophets—especially of those who predicted the Exile and the destruction of Israel and Judah. The books of the prophets Jeremiah and Habakkuk have much to say about suffering, and one of the major themes in the prophetic books of the Old Testament concerns the necessity of suffering among the prophets: their persecution, ostracism and ill treatment at the hands of others. In the first chapter of Jeremiah, God sees fit to warn the prophet about his enemies: "Do not be afraid of them, for I am with you to deliver you, says the Lord" (Jer 1:8). The prophet Ezekiel is also told that the people will make his life difficult: "And you, O mortal, do not be afraid of them, and do not be afraid of their words, though briers and thorns surround you and you live among scorpions; do not be afraid of their words, and do not be dismayed at their looks, for they are a rebellious house. You shall speak my words to them, whether they hear or refuse to hear; for they are a rebellious house" (Ezek 2:6–7). This prophetic suffering seems to be both unjust and yet linked to the preaching of justice: the sufferings of

Jeremiah and Ezekiel are paradoxically both contrary to God's will and part of God's plan.

It is not surprising therefore to find that about one third of the Psalms constitute cries to God that arise out of doubt, disappointment or pain.

And lastly, of course, one of the larger books of the Old Testament is the Book of Job. It is entirely given over to a debate and consideration of the question of suffering—and in particular, the suffering of a righteous person who did nothing to deserve his suffering . . . We return to this later on.

───

As we look carefully at the Old Testament, we also see that it does not speak with one voice about suffering. There is an internal dialogue, a debate, an argument over the causes and meaning of suffering. The book of Deuteronomy, and the so-called "deuteronomic history" books—Joshua, Judges, Samuel and Kings, go for a simple—many would say a simplistic—solution. Suffering comes to people because God is punishing them for their sins. As Michael Thompson says in his excellent book *Where is the God of justice?* "The point is made that as long as the people walk in God's ways, and obey his commandments and ordinances, then all will go well with them."[1] The much repeated refrain of the book goes like this: "You must therefore be careful to do as the Lord your God has commanded you; you shall not turn to the right or to the left. You must follow exactly the path that the Lord your God has commanded you, so that you may live, and that it may go well with you, and that you may live long in the land that you are to possess" (Deut 5:32–33). In chapter 30 (vv. 15–20), Moses exhorts the people to choose between good and evil, between life and death. If they choose the way of God, and life, all will go well, but if they choose other gods or their own way, that way will lead to spiritual death, a shortened life and things will not go well.

All the kings of Israel and Judah are judged according to this golden rule. If they obey God's commands, they are commended and the kingdom is seen to thrive and flourish. If they go whoring after other gods, then things go badly with the kingdom. A powerful king like Omri is dismissed peremptorily because he did what was evil in the sight of the Lord. A good king like Hezekiah served the Lord and thus God made him prosper. He defeated his enemies and refused to serve foreign kings or foreign deities (2 Kgs 18:5–8). King Josiah of Judah is also commended, because he worshipped Yahweh, reformed the worship of the Temple and also introduced a new law book—probably the book of Deuteronomy itself! He "put away the mediums, wizards, teraphim and all the abominations that were seen

---

1. Thompson, *Where is the God of Justice*, 8.

in the land of Judah" (2 Kgs 23:24). All went well with Josiah and he was a much-revered king. However, he was killed in battle half way through his reforming work, and suddenly the writer of Deuteronomy goes silent. There is no explanation as to why an upright and godly king could be cut off in his prime ... This does not fit well with the theology of the book.

By way of contrast, the fall of the northern kingdom of Israel to the Assyrian hordes (722 BC) is easily explained: the kings and the people had sinned against God, had taken to worshipping other gods and had married foreign women and had acted immorally and unjustly. They deserved their fate. As it says in 2 Kings 17:22-23: "The people of Israel continued in all the sins that Jeroboam committed; they did not depart from them until the Lord removed Israel out of his sight ... And so Israel was exiled from their own land to Assyria until this day." Later on, the same fate of exile falls upon the kingdom of Judah when the Babylonians invaded (587 BC) and the writer pronounces the same judgement as before: "I am bringing upon Jerusalem and Judah such evil that everyone who hears of it will tingle ... I will ... give them into the hands of their enemies; they shall become a prey and a spoil to their enemies, because they have done what is evil in my sight and have provoked me to anger"(2 Kgs 21:12, 14-15).

Thus, the deuteronomic writer has it that faithfulness to God leads to success but sinfulness leads to disaster—even the absolute disaster of deportation and exile; the loss of the promised land, all possessions and even the Temple—the House of God—in Jerusalem.

The strange thing about Deuteronomy and the deuteronomic history is that there is a detached, dispassionate tone to the judgements. The author does not seem to share in or sympathise with the sufferings of his people. This is no longer the case when we read the Book of Lamentations and the Psalms of lament. Even though there is still a similar, somewhat simplistic theology of sin causing suffering, nevertheless now the predominant tone is the sense of distress brought about by the reality of terrible suffering. The writer complains bitterly of his own fate: "Is it nothing to you who pass by? Look and see if there is any sorrow like my sorrow, which was brought upon me, which the Lord inflicted on the day of his fierce anger" (Lam 1:12). These words are immortalized in Handel's Messiah. Of the fate of the people in general, the writer only has words of anguish and sorrow: "The Lord has become like an enemy; he has destroyed Israel. He has destroyed all its palaces, laid in ruins its strongholds, and multiplied in daughter Judah mourning and lamentation" (2:5). And yet although God is deemed to be directly responsible for Israel's devastation, the author is still determined to praise God and recognize his goodness and justice: "The steadfast love of the Lord never ceases, his mercies never come to an end; they are new every morning; great is your faithfulness. The Lord is my portion, says my soul, therefore I will hope in him" (3:22–24).

We are happy to use these famous words in our liturgy, but do not say them in the same context of total destruction and the deportation and humiliation of God's own people. In some sense, the writer of Lamentations still clings to the deuteronomic idea that the calamities falling upon Israel and Judah are the result of sin—either that of an individual (maybe the king), a group (perhaps the religious or secular elite) or of the whole people. For that reason God's judgement has fallen and has even affected the innocent. This is a great and traumatic shock, according to the writer, but, in spite of this, the contention is that God's anger will not last for ever, and that he still remains the God of justice and mercy.

Whatever their theology, the given fact that Old Testament writers accepted without question was that God was a God of integrity and righteousness. However, as time went on, the response to suffering which asserts that it is directly caused by sin came to be questioned. This was largely because criminals and self-seeking individuals were sometimes seen to flourish with impunity, and secondly because events did not turn out as they ought to in a moral Universe.

The Psalmists often pose the leading question, "Why do the wicked prosper?" In Psalm 73, for example, the writer admits, "I was envious of the arrogant; I saw the prosperity of the wicked" (v. 3) and he goes on to describe the good life of the unrighteous: "They have no pain, their bodies are sound and sleek. They are not in trouble as others are . . . Pride is their necklace; violence covers them like a garment. Their eyes swell out with fatness . . . They scoff and speak with malice; loftily they threaten oppression. They set their mouths against heaven, and their tongues range over the earth" (vv. 4–9). Here is a severe case of jealousy, even bitterness, and the response is to cling to God. His counsels are good and his guidance is sound. But the Psalmist demonstrates that real experience often goes against the notion that crime does not pay, that the sinful life will never succeed. Experience shows us a different scenario—the wicked often get away with it and things do not go as God planned. As James Crenshaw says in his recent book: "Historical events . . . frequently took perplexing turns that defied systematization. The deuteronomic understanding of strict reward and retribution . . . was difficult to reconcile with the real-life experience of Yahweh's people."[2] So the experiences of real life led some among God's people to search for a better understanding of God's ways.

---

2. Crenshaw, *Defending God*, 76.

We find such a response to real life experience in the Book of Job.

The Book of Job is not an easy read. Yet it is the one clear examination of the central question; how can God allow a good and righteous person to suffer and fail? The book has Job's friends Eliphaz, Bildad and Zophar build a case against him; not with one cycle of speeches, but three! And then, as though that were not enough, we have the long-winded contribution of Elihu. If Job were not crushed enough by misfortune, the so-called "comforters" try to load a great burden of guilt upon him with unsympathetic accusations throughout! Not only that, but even at the end, the Book of Job does not come up with any clear solution to the problem of innocent suffering.

The Prologue sets the scene and tells us about the disastrous change of fortune experienced by Job, who with his wealth and possessions was "the greatest of all the people of the east" (1:3). Not only that, but he was blessed with a faithful wife, seven sons, three daughters and many servants. The introductory passage makes crystal clear that Job was "blameless and upright, one who feared God and turned away from evil." Thus, the normal explanation of his afflictions will not suffice—for Job has it that those who live devout and upright lives and who worship God devotedly do not always receive their just desserts. In fact, Job loses everything. Satan, the adversary sitting in God's council, is allowed to bring a curse upon Job and remove all the blessings he had hitherto enjoyed: the animals were stolen in raids or burnt alive, his sons and daughters were killed by a whirlwind and Job's body was covered with loathsome sores and he lost his good health. The trial perhaps takes away the full responsibility for inflicted extreme cruelty by introducing the "satan" who wants to test Job's faith to the uttermost in order to prove that he will deny God in his extremity. This "satan" accusing and undermining believers is a late entrant into the Old Testament narrative and shows that the Book of Job is a late composition. The story itself also reads like a carefully constructed piece of literature designed to state its case in terms which allow no gray areas theologically. The writing is often wonderfully poetic and a model of clarity, and has many features of the Wisdom literature of the Near East.

Job's so-called "friends" start out well but finish badly. At first they sat with him on the ground for seven days and seven nights and had sympathy in silence, "for they saw that his suffering was very great" (2:13).Then after this Job "opened his mouth and cursed the day of his birth." His life is in tatters and his mind is in turmoil. Then the "friends" began to embark upon their different but rather too similar "explanations" of Job's sufferings, which largely amounted to the view that he could not be as good as he thought—he must have sinned and should repent. And he should not be so proud as to imagine that he was blameless in the sight of God.

Eliphaz, the leader of the "friends" expresses the two-pronged attack in this way: first, he says to Job, "Think now, who that was innocent ever perished? Or where were the upright cut off? As I understand it, those who plough iniquity and sow trouble will reap the same and by the breath of God they perish" (4:7–8). So this is the old adage, you reap what you sow. And then secondly, Eliphaz attacks Job's pride in his own blameless life: "Can mortals be righteous before God? Can human beings be pure before their Maker? Even in his servants he puts no trust, and his angels he charges with error" (4:17–18).

Eliphaz adds something to the debate by arguing that suffering can be seen as a way in which God disciplines his servants and strengthens character. "How happy is the one whom God reproves; therefore do not despise the discipline of the Almighty" (5:17). Later on, Elihu, in the final speeches, takes up this same theme at length (chs. 32—37).

Elihu also has another new point, which is taken up at the end of the Book of Job, when God himself responds to Job. Elihu challenges Job by asking him if he really understands what is involved in creating a world like this: a world full of wonders, but also a world with moral choice and freedom:

> Do you know how God lays his command upon them,
> and causes the lightning of his cloud to shine?
> Do you know the balancings of the clouds,
> The wondrous works of the one whose knowledge is perfect?
> You whose garments are hot when the earth is still because of the south wind?
> Can you, like him, spread out the skies,
> unyielding as a cast mirror? (Job 37:15–18)

This lays the groundwork for God's reply to Job in the following chapter, and we will come to that. Suffice it to say here that Elihu is not simply pointing out the glories of nature, but is hinting at something far deeper: that this world, even with its terrible suffering, is the world which gives human beings freedom, adventure and awesome experiences.

Job, in his responses, begins by venting his anger. He regards his friends as great betrayers: for they "are treacherous as the rapids in a river, like seasonal streams that pass away" (6:15 my translation). But Job is also angry with *God*: has he not given human beings a hard life "like the days of a laborer, like a slave who longs for the shadow" (7:1–2). And further, life can even be devoid of hope: Job's suffering includes mental distress: "I am allotted months of emptiness, and nights of misery are apportioned to me."

Life's days "come to their end without hope" (7:3, 6). Job feels isolated and alone. The contest between him and God is unequal and he needs an umpire to sympathize and to present his case (see 9:32–35).

Later on, in chapter 12, Job has a more positive speech in praise of God's wisdom: "With God are wisdom and strength; he has counsel and understanding" (12:13). This is seen in the ways of the birds and animals and in the order of creation. Such is not the case for Job's "friends" who make wrong judgements and will not be silent. Job longs for one who will be sympathetic and kindly. If God has been cruel and harsh, who can come alongside him to help him? It seems though that God might take this role too, He might have allowed "the slings and arrows of outrageous fortune" to be directed at Job, but he might also be the one who listens to Job's complaints, who answers Job's pleas, who comes alongside him: As Job says, "I know that my Redeemer lives, and that at the last he will stand upon the earth, and after my skin has thus been destroyed, then in my flesh I shall see God, whom I shall see on my side" (Job 19:25–27). This is something of a breakthrough for Job and this aspect of the debate is developed in the final chapters, when God reveals himself in dramatic fashion to reassure Job, and also to challenge his earlier lack of faith. Michael Thompson explains this new revelation to Job in a lucid manner, when he writes:

> Job, in these words, is portrayed as experiencing something remarkable.
>
> It is nothing less than his coming to a new vision of God, coming to understand that God may after all be one who is present with him, not merely far away from him. It is as if he has come to know for himself that the almighty and illimitable God, the transcendent One, as well as being transcendent, can also be for his people immanent and immediate to them in their deep needs and sufferings.[3]

Job begins a new relationship with God at this point. He now sees God as being "on his side" or, to put it another way, his "witness in heaven," the one who vouches for him (16:19). This new insight not only gives Job new hope, but makes his heart faint within him, as he puts it in 19:27.

We hear from Job again in 21:1–34, but little new is added. However, in his contribution to the long speech running from 23:1 to 24:25, Job in a sense returns to the theme we have just outlined: that of Job longing to see God and putting his case to him: "Oh, that I knew where I might find him, that I might come even to his dwelling! I would lay my case before him,

---

3. Thompson, *Where is the God of Justice?*, 132.

and fill my mouth with arguments" (23:3–4). Then Job goes on to utter his old complaint; that the wicked and godless seem to have carefree, happy lives despite oppressing and harming others. But in this long speech, and in the next (26:1—27:6) Job is very much aware of the stupendous power of God, whom to see is, for a human, both terrifying and awesome. In this later speech, Job is beginning to have a sense of his own smallness and insignificance.

In chapter 28 of Job we have a chapter dedicated to the praise of Wisdom. This stands out from all the preceding chapters, but it nevertheless links up with the issues with which the book as a whole is dealing. This chapter is written not as argument or disputation, but as an elevated piece of Hebrew poetry. It gives the reader pause and time to reflect upon the best—and wisest way—to live life in a fragmented, confusing and sometimes hostile world. The passage begins with a detailed description of the skill and ingenuity human beings display in being able to mine precious metals and stones from the earth. Yet, the passage goes on, this kind of earthly wisdom pales in comparison with the wisdom emanating from God and present in the mind of God. Thus, the conclusion is that true wisdom will only be found and gained when sought in God, the source of all understanding. Because God has created all things, put them in their place and ordered them, he is the only one who comprehends everything under heaven, including knowing the difference between good and evil.

How do these insights then affect our response to the suffering of the innocent? First of all, much suffering can be avoided through wise choices in life, and especially if evil ways are shunned. Second, knowing God and seeking wisdom in God can give reassurance and perseverance to a person who is actually suffering: "Truly, the fear of the Lord, that is wisdom; and to depart from evil, that is understanding" (28:28). Thirdly, meaning in life and coming to terms with suffering is not granted through theological argument, however sophisticated, but rather in reverence for and worship of God. The presence of God brings both wisdom and comfort.

Job's final speech runs from 29:1 to 31:40 and follows directly from the poem in praise of wisdom. Job's intention in this last plea is to put his case clearly before God and to persuade God to have sympathy for him, the innocent sufferer. Then the rather self-important speeches of Elihu follow on. He proudly seems to appoint himself as an arbiter between Job and God, and argues that God is disciplining Job and refining his character through a kind of trial by fire. Elihu also points out to Job some of the grandeur of God's works and God's ways. (e.g. 37. 14—19). In this, he acts as a warm-up or preparation for the great outpouring that follows—the response of God himself.

Chapters 38 and 39 (40:2) are presented as a divine theophany, God answers Job "out of the whirlwind." This is the very thing Job had been longing for. But it is not the *vindication* that Job was expecting or hoping for. It does not offer an explanation for Job's suffering, nor a validation of his righteousness. On the contrary, it is more of a rebuke to Job, that he has not trusted God enough or rested in God through all his suffering. Job has not looked around him enough to appreciate the mighty and wondrous works of God in creation.

Thus, Job is not offered a rational explanation about why he had to suffer. Instead, he has first to realize his own smallness and limitations. He is not the one who laid the foundations of the earth. He did not command the morning to appear. He did not enter the springs of the sea or find his way to the source of the light. Some knowledge is far beyond his ken. Besides, the knowledge of God is not just a rational explanation of life; it is an experience of transcendence and overwhelming glory. So, in the wake of such an experience, Job's response in no longer a complaint; it is a humble submission to God.

> Then Job answered the Lord: "See, I am of small account, what shall I answer You? I lay my hand upon my mouth. I have spoken once and I will not answer" (Job 40:4–5).

Job has been overwhelmed by the manifestation of God's "shekinah"—his radiant presence—and at the same time, he has been satisfied, he is now content because he has seen God and had his prayers answered.

But God has not yet finished. There is another long speech to come, and this one is more mysterious than the first. Now God asks Job, what do you know about two fearsome creatures, Behemoth and Leviathan? The former—Behemoth (40:15–24) is a huge land creature with great strength. He was one of God's first and fiercest creations and only God can approach it (v. 19). It is beyond human strength to capture or master it. The second creature, Leviathan (41:1–34)—is evidently a sea-going monster of such size that it cannot be caught or controlled by human beings. It is fearful and terrifying, breathing out fire and smoke (41:18–21).

What is the significance of these two creatures and why is a chapter of Job taken up with their description? Does their size and power graphically highlight the even greater power of God as their creator? Perhaps so, but this is not the main point. The main idea is probably that Behemoth and Leviathan represent the great superhuman forces of nature unleashed in the world—sometimes forces that threaten and destroy. Yet, mysteriously, these forces, while sometimes allowed to cause some havoc, are still under the supervision and control of God. They will not be allowed to run amok and destroy the basic order of God's creation. Leviathan is representative of those evil forces which disrupt the natural harmony of God's world, but they—like Leviathan—will be defeated on the Day of the Lord by the Lord himself. Their time—like that of evil and self-serving men who do well in this life—is limited. They will be judged and put in their place in the end.

The battle between God and Leviathan at the time of creation is described in Psalm 74:14, where Leviathan is tamed to some extent, and the monster's doom is cast from that time onwards. Yet God's complete victory over the forces of evil will only be fully accomplished *in the future* when sin and evil are banished from creation. Behemoth is also regarded as a great force of evil; appearing in the apocalyptic literature between the testaments and in books like 1 Enoch and 4 Esdras. In the Apocalypse of Baruch, these two creatures are linked together as mythical enemies of God in the End Times.

So by the use of the examples of Leviathan and Behemoth, the Book of Job demonstrates to us that while there are malign and even evil forces in the world striving against God's purposes, which cause great suffering in the present, their power—and their time—are limited. They are—despite appearances—under God's authority, subject to his will, and their nefarious machinations will only be allowed to continue until the present world conditions come to an end. So the final section of Job is not so much a strange and fanciful story of fictional beasts: it is a poetic way of saying that while we do not understand fully the reasons that God allows evil to hold sway at times and affect people's lives, nonetheless God has actually put a restraint on such destructive activity and will eventually destroy it.

In his book *Faith and Wisdom in Science*, Tom McLeish, Professor of Physics in the University of Durham, has an interesting take on the conclusion of the Book of Job:

> The message of Job is that chaos is part of the fruitfulness of creation; we cannot hope to control it any more than we can bridle Leviathan, but by understanding we might channel it. Indeed, new structures can arise when we do—the beginning of wisdom is not to double-lock the casket of our ignorance, but to "seek the fear of the Lord," where this is understood to be a participation in a creator's deep insight into the structure of what he has made . . . situating our science and technology within a story of participative healing.[4]

Professor McLeish is perhaps moving towards the conclusion that the best way to cope with suffering and evil in life is to remain faithful to God. The

---

4. McLeish, *Faith and Wisdom in Science*, 256.

alternative—denying and defying God—makes suffering completely pointless and destroys our soul in bitterness.

At the end of the book, Job seems to have come to an understanding. He is now reconciled with God. But he is also ashamed of his lack of trust and his rebellious spirit. Now, after sitting in ashes at the beginning (2:8) bemoaning his fate, he sits again in ashes, but for a very different reason: "I had heard you by the hearing of the ear," says Job, "but now my eye sees you; therefore I despise myself and repent in dust and ashes." The Book of Job does not finish with God justifying his ways through rational argument. Rather, it finishes by showing that God is real and aware of Job's suffering, drawing close to Job in order to reassure him and bring him comfort. And finally, God explains in a picturesque way that he holds sway over the whole of creation and that he intends to hold evil in check and eventually to defeat and banish sin and evil from the world.

One other thing needs to be said about God's final speech. The theology of Job's three friends, the deuteronomic, simplistic theology that the righteous are rewarded and sinners are punished; that theology is condemned outright. God tells Job that these friends have exhibited "folly" (*nebala*, 42:8) and have not spoken rightly or truly about God. Only Job himself has spoken the truth. (42:7-8). The sufferings of Job are not due to his sinfulness: Job did not "deserve" his sufferings. So the book ends with God restoring Job's fortunes and giving him twice as much as he had before (42:10).

The final position of the Book of Job is that the answer to the world's suffering is not to be found in any rational theodicy—although it is worth saying that rational argument is important as a first stage of reasoning about life. Thus, someone who rejects God because of the world's suffering has to rationally explain away the order, beauty, harmony, regularity and mathematical precision displayed in the Universe, as we have already seen in the first section. But in the end no purely rational explanation is enough. The palliative to the problem of suffering is to be found—paradoxically—in the worship of God, in reverence and trust. Through this lifestyle God can draw near, show his compassion and reassure the sufferer of his willingness to draw alongside and help. God is truly "God with us": he has an interest in human life and in individual lives. But more than that, we can also be reassured that suffering and all concomitant evils are contrary to the will of God, and will, to some degree, be held in check, and then ultimately will be destroyed in the end. There will be a time when wrongs are righted and justice is seen to be done. This does not go so far as to say that suffering can have a purpose; this insight comes with the prophet Isaiah and his figure of the suffering servant of God, and it is to this we now turn.

CHAPTER FOUR

THE SUFFERING SERVANT OF ISAIAH

ALTHOUGH SCHOLARS NOWADAYS OFTEN treat Isaiah as a single literary composition, with themes recurring and developing throughout, nevertheless, in principle the book we know can be split into three sections, with each relating to a different period in the history of Israel. The first part, chapters 1—39, fits the context of the eighth century BC, and there are similarities between this early section and other early written prophets, like Amos, Hosea and Micah. Jumping to the final part of Isaiah, the third section, chapters 55—66, this is thought to be written by disciples of the early prophet and the author of the middle section, chapters 40—54. Whereas the middle part is written towards the end of the exile in Babylon, the final part is addressed to those who are back in Jerusalem, attempting to rebuild the Temple and the city walls.

We are now concerned with the middle part of Isaiah, often known as Second Isaiah (or Deutero-Isaiah), This is a great poetic work, filled with the hope of liberation and the end of exile. Babylon is soon to be conquered by King Cyrus and his Persian army. After a spectacular series of victories in battle, he entered Babylon in 539 BC. Cyrus was to bring greater toleration of different minority religions across his empire—including Judaism. He later allowed the Jews to return to their ancient homeland and to take back the Temple treasures to Jerusalem in readiness to rebuild the Temple.

Second Isaiah contains some of the noblest religious ideals found in the whole of the Old Testament. The central idea is that God will prove himself to be the liberator and vindicator of his people and will lead them out of captivity in a second Exodus. The prophet is a thoroughgoing monotheist, regarding God as the Lord of all creation and of all peoples. Other gods were nothing more than man-made idols or figments of the imagination. The writer—like many Old Testament prophets—sees the Jewish people as chosen by God, but separated out not to enjoy special privileges or to look down on other nations, but for the task of serving all people, witnessing to the reality of the true God, teaching others of him, and taking their knowledge and love of God to the four corners of the earth.

The really radical idea of Second Isaiah, however, is that Israel might have to suffer in order to achieve her vocation. This suffering should not be regarded as punishment for sins; rather, it is a redemptive suffering on behalf of others, to bring great benefits to them. This remarkable concept of suffering is best seen in the so-called Servant Songs of Isaiah chapters 42:1-4; 49:1-6; 50:4-9 and 52:13—53:12. The figure portrayed in these poetic stanzas is commonly known as "the suffering servant."

To a disheartened people, Isaiah has God crying out to the prophet, "Comfort, O comfort my people! Speak tenderly to Jerusalem and tell her that she has served her term; her penalty is paid. But she will receive double (blessing) for all her sins."(40:1-2). Then a voice cries out in the wilderness urging the people of God to prepare a road through the wilderness, to make a straight highway for God to lead the people out. The people are to see the glory of the Lord, as in the days of the Exodus from Egypt (40:3-5). God has not forsaken his people during the exile; far from it—he intends to take them home and to restore their fortunes The rise and fall of Babylon is, to God, a small thing. He watches all empires rise and fall, as their pride and hubris gives way to shame and humiliation.

Enclosed within the bright and joyful news of release and liberation are the dark shadows of the Servant Songs—sombre passages about unjust suffering. These strike a discordant note in the surrounding material. Not only are the Servant Songs dark and solemn; they are also mysterious and enigmatic. Scholars have struggled to arrive at a common mind regarding their true meaning. Who is the suffering servant of God? Is it Israel as a whole? But then why should Israel have to face more suffering after all that time in exile? Could it perhaps be a representative of Israel? Someone whose suffering and tribulations bring redemption and freedom to the rest of the people. Perhaps this could even be the prophet himself. Or could it be a messianic figure? One who will come to restore Israel's greatness and independence through his willingness to suffer for his godly mission. Who then did the author have in mind when he wrote the Servant Songs?

The puzzle deepens when we consider that the first two passages on the Servant are *not* about suffering at all! (Isa 42:1-4 and 49:1-6). Rather, they are about one who has a great mission to bring the knowledge of God to a wider world. In the first passage, the servant is one in whom God delights, who is given the power of God's Spirit, who will bring justice to the nations. What is so remarkable about this passage is that the servant is not a warrior king in the mould of king David, nor a conquering hero in the mould of king Cyrus. Instead, we have a figure who, softly spoken and gentle, who champions the downtrodden and those bruised by life: "a bruised reed he will not break, and a dimly burning wick he will not quench" (42:3). He is nevertheless determined to succeed in his mission and will persevere until the end in his quest to bring justice for all—especially the poor.

And so two great themes begin to emerge here: first, that God wishes his people—and especially his servant—to reach out to the whole world with a message of peace and justice. God, for Second Isaiah, is the God of all people. Second, the servant must spread God's word peaceably and gently and not impose his will in a warlike or violent manner. In this way, the servant is to be "a covenant to the people" (in this case, to Israel), and "a light to the nations" (42:6-7). This mission will "open the eyes of the blind" and "bring out of prison those who sit in darkness" (42:7). This is a new thing God is bringing into being—a new message and a new mission, spearheaded by his servant.

The second passage (49:1-6) puts the words of the servant into the prophet's own mouth: "The Lord has called me before I was born; while I was still in my mother's womb he named me" (49:1). The servant's words will now be like "a sharp sword" or "a polished arrow" (v. 2)—words with a cutting edge and power. His task is to bring Israel back to her true vocation; and this is in fact for a great purpose: to reach out to all the nations. Once again, the servant is called to be "a light to the nations" (49:6). God's intention now is to offer salvation to all who turn to him or who will hear the message. This is a radical dramatic ideal; for the people of Israel had, for many years, been oppressed under cruel empires (namely, Assyria and Babylon), and had struggled to maintain their identity in the face of persecution and pressure. They surely had many reasons to resent and avoid the Gentiles, far from reaching out to them with a message of God's love and mercy.

When we reach the third Servant Song (50:4-9), we then learn of the necessity of the servant's suffering. His mission is bound to incur a great personal cost. Once again, the prophet takes on the role and words of the servant. The servant now becomes "the teacher" (50:4), but his teachings must give great offence, because he is struck on the back and his beard is pulled in an insulting manner (v.6); he is also insulted and spat upon. Who are these enemies of the servant, and why do his words cause such outrage?

It seems that the message about God and the call to repentance and to a new way of living invite antagonism and indignation, in the same way as in many of the Psalms "the enemies" of the author threaten and oppose the words and works of the Psalmist—mainly because they react to the godly way of life and because they are unwilling to hear God's word or obey it. This theme runs like a golden thread throughout Scripture. It is not only prominent in the Psalms, but also in the prophetic writings. When Jeremiah is sent to preach and prophesy to the people, he is fearful of the effect his words will have and of the suffering he will have to undergo because of his commitment to the Word of God. The Lord commands him and cajoles him, but also reassures him:

> Do not say "I am only a boy." You shall go to all to whom I send you and you shall speak whatever I command you. Do not be afraid of them, for I am with you to deliver you, says the Lord" (Jer 1:7–8).

Just a little later, the Lord has to warn Jeremiah of the people's hostility and threats:

> "Do not break down before them . . . I for my part have made you today a fortified city, an iron pillar and a bronze wall, against the whole land—against the kings of Judah, its princes, its priests, and the people of the land. They will fight against you, but they shall not prevail against you, for I am with you, says the Lord, to deliver you" (Jer 1:17–19).

In a sense, this theme reaches its apotheosis in the first chapter of John's gospel, when the Word of God is incarnated in Jesus Christ. He came into the world he created, "not to condemn the world but that it might be saved through him" (John 3:17), "but the world did not know him. He came into his own, but his own people did not accept him" (John 1:17–19).

So it is very clear that taking the message—the Word of God—to Israel or to the nations as a whole—is a dangerous and risky venture, bound to lead to suffering and rejection. The challenge of God's Word to those who cling to power and prestige, to the rich and complacent, to the absentee landlord extorting high rents, to the oppressive employer paying low wages, to the violent miscreant—this challenge meets with resistance, opposition and sometimes violence.

The fourth and final Servant Song of Isaiah is found in chapter 52 verse 13 to chapter 53 verse 12. The themes which appeared earlier return and recur, but are deepened and taken in new directions.

The first section is 52:13–15, which actually begins on a very positive note. God's servant, if he carries out his commission, will be honored and rewarded: "He shall be exalted and lifted up, and shall be very high" (52:11). But immediately after this we have a picture of the servant's degrading treatment at the hands of others: "Many were astonished at him—so marred was his appearance, beyond human semblance, and his form beyond that of mortals" (52:14). This puzzling turn-around is maintained at the beginning of chapter 53, where we read that the servant "had no form or majesty that we should look at him, nothing in his appearance that we should desire him," but then we discover the reason for the great alteration in his appearance: "He was despised and rejected by others; a man of suffering and acquainted with infirmity" (53:4).

The account of the servant's suffering then becomes more and more horrific—and it is compounded by the fact that no one understands or sympathizes: "We accounted him stricken, struck down by God, and afflicted, yet he did not open his mouth. By a perversion of justice he was taken away . . . He was cut off from the land of the living, stricken for the transgressions of my people. They made his grave with the wicked" (53:7–9).

The people who witnessed this blamed God for his sufferings . . . Yet the remarkable twist in the story is the prophet's insistence that the people were responsible and that the servant was innocent: "He had done no violence, and there was no deceit in his mouth" (v. 9). Nevertheless, he had to suffer *because of us*—and yet his suffering brought blessing and benefits to us and gave rise to our healing:

> Surely he has borne our infirmities and carried our diseases . . . He was wounded for our transgressions, crushed for our iniquities. Upon him was the punishment that made us whole, and by his bruises we are healed (53:5).

It transpires that the sins of the people (the "our" and "us" of the passage) could be remitted and forgiven by means of the servant's suffering. The diseases and sicknesses of the people could be healed by his afflictions and agonies.

⌇

Even though this man—the servant—was innocent and free of any evildoing, he was condemned as a sinner and he suffered as a criminal. The judgement of God seemed to be upon him, but, as the prophet makes clear, the judgement that fell on him should have fallen on "us."

Is this some sort of "exchange," whereby the sins of the many are transferred to the one—the suffering servant? Is that one person seeking purposely to receive the punishment due to others? Does he substitute himself for sinners, that they might be acquitted? Can the freely offered life of an innocent man preserve or restore the life of many others?

To speak in more religious terms, is this a kind of sacrifice offered to God for the sins or guilt of the people? Does the innocent man act as a scapegoat? This last is a ritual sacrifice well known to the people of Israel and to be found in Leviticus 16. In a special ceremony on the Day of Atonement, the sins of all the people were prayed for by the High Priest, who would enter the Holy of Holies in the Temple—on that day only—to make a sacrifice of one goat—called the sin offering of the Lord—and he would pray that God might forgive and lay aside the sins of all the people for the year past. A second goat would then be chosen, who was named Azazel (perhaps after a demon). Symbolically the sins of Israel would be transferred to that goat through prayers of confession, and the goat would then be chased away into the wilderness, carrying the sins of the people on his back. He was sent far from the habitations of humanity and was known as "the scapegoat." The hope was that with his expulsion the sins of Israel too could be expelled from the land. This would be the nearest thing to an Old Testament understanding of atonement.

In Isaiah 53 the suffering servant appears very much to be a scapegoat; one who can atone for the sins of many people. He is in this way like a sin offering.

But in verse 12, we find that the suffering servant of God "also made intercession for the transgressors." In this way he was acting more like the High Priest. Now these two roles are not mutually contradictory. In the New Testament, Jesus himself is viewed both as the one perfect sacrifice for sin and also (in *The Letter to the Hebrews*) as the model High Priest who makes intercession for the sins of the people. So if a sacrificial offering is one way to achieve the forgiveness of sins, intercessory prayer is another.

Solomon prayed for the forgiveness of his people in 1 Kings chapter 8 when the new Temple was being consecrated and dedicated as God's house. Earlier in the Old Testament, Abraham prayed for God's mercy towards the people of Sodom, for the sake of the small number of righteous folk living there (Gen 18:23–33). Moses prayed to God for the forgiveness of Israel's sins after the making of the golden calf which was then worshipped as a god (Exod 32:11-13; 31–32 and Deut 9:18–21). The prophet Amos is also portrayed as praying to God for a sinful nation in Amos 7:1–6. So there is a strong and well known tradition in Israel's history that righteous people, or people in a special position of authority (High Priest, King, Prophet) could use intercessory prayer to plead with God on behalf of the assembly of Israel, and could even prevail and persuade God to relent and perhaps to change his mind.

A modern example of intercession, which parallels the case of the suffering servant of Isaiah, comes from the experience of C.S. Lewis, at a time when his wife was stricken with cancer and suffering a great deal. The story is told that as his wife Joy lay stricken and nearing her death, Lewis prayed to God that he might take away some of his wife's pain and take it into his own body. For several minutes following that prayer, he felt a terrible pain in his legs, which lasted for several minutes. A look of relief simultaneously came over Joy's face. There was some kind of answer to Lewis's intercessory prayer which allowed him—through faith—to share in his wife's agonies.

Perhaps it is true to say that something similar transpired when Jesus was in the Garden of Gethsemane. He was "grieved and agitated" (Matt 26:37) and he prayed in anguish. We read that his sweat was "like great drops of blood falling down on the ground" (Luke 22:44). He somehow came to know something of the burden and torment of human sin even before the cross.

Then there is a third possible interpretation of the purpose and achievement of the suffering servant—after sacrifice for sin and intercessory prayer—and that is that the actions of the servant have a vicarious effect; that is, they deliver benefits through the deliberate acceptance of suffering on behalf of others.

At a much later date than the writings of Second Isaiah, the martyrs of the Maccabean revolt (against the Greek rulers of the time—167-160 BC) were regarded as individuals whose righteous deaths would bring great benefits to the rest of the people of Israel.

A modern example of vicarious suffering would be that of Maximilian Kolbe, from the Second World War. A Polish Franciscan priest, Kolbe was arrested in February 1941 by the Nazis for publishing unapproved literature. He was sentenced to hard labor at the Auschwitz concentration camp. Later that year, a prisoner in the camp escaped. He was not recaptured, and so the camp guards decided to take reprisals, in order to deter other prisoners from trying to escape. They lined the prisoners up and randomly chose ten men to be sent to a starvation bunker to endure a slow and painful death. At this point, one prisoner, a farmer called Franciszek Gajowniczek, cried out in despair, "My wife, my children!" On hearing this pitiful cry, Maximilian Kolbe stepped out of the line. He told the guard, "I am a Catholic priest with no family. Let me take the place of this man." The guard hesitated, then agreed to Kolbe's altruistic request. The nine others went, with Kolbe accompanying them, to the starvation bunker. After fourteen days, four were still alive, including Father Kolbe. The Nazis then decided to inject the four remaining with carbolic acid, so that their deaths would be hastened.

Thirty years later, Pope Paul VI declared that Maximilian Kolbe was to be beatified—often a step on the way to sainthood. At the ceremony, next to the Pope stood Franciszek Gajowniczek. He had survived the concentration camp, rejoined his family and had spent his life telling others what Father Kolbe had done for him; how he had died in the place of another, to give him, Franciszek, new life and release.

━━

How did Isaiah himself understand the sufferings of the servant of God? There is certainly *an element of sacrifice* involved: "The Lord has laid on him the iniquity of us all" (53:6). With these words, as Michael Thompson says, "he intended to bring to our minds the ritual of the scapegoat about which we read in Leviticus 16."[1] In other words, the powers and effects of sin were being transferred from the people to the sacrificial offering, and those sins were to be taken far away from the people—out of sight and out of mind.

There is also *an element of intercession* involved: "He bore the sin of many and made intercession for the transgressors" (53:12). Many people have experienced the struggle of praying for others. It is often draining and hard work. It requires real empathy and a placing of oneself in the situation of others. No true intercessory prayer is achieved without a certain "taking on" of the sufferings of others.

In the gospels, Jesus provides a clear example of this. During his ministry, the healing of the sick through intercessory prayer often left him exhausted. In the case of the woman who had been bleeding for twelve years (Mark 5:25-34 and parallels), when she approached Jesus apprehensively and touched his cloak, she was convinced that he could make her well: he was a man full of God's Spirit. Her hemorrhaging did stop, but Jesus very obviously sensed her action. "Power had gone forth from him" (Mark 5:30). The disciples responded by saying that many people had pressed up against him. However, Jesus had noticed that some healing power had drained away from him, and that this had had a powerful effect on the woman. She then came forward in fear and trembling, falling down before him (5:33). She had taken power from Jesus without permission and without entering into a relationship with Jesus or with God. Yet Jesus simply said, without condemnation, "Daughter, your faith has made you well. Go in peace and be healed of your disease" (5:34).

Thirdly, and finally, there is also *an element of vicarious suffering* in the servant's willingness to take the place of others: "He has borne *our* infirmities and carried *our* diseases . . . He was wounded for *our* transgressions and crushed for *our* iniquities" (53:4-5). This does not mean, as some might argue, that the servant *becomes a sinner* as well as a sufferer. This is not a "substitutionary atonement" *avant la lettre*. Rather, it is a willingness to undergo

---

1. Thompson. *Where is the God of Justice?*, 95.

suffering *on behalf of* someone else. It may be that he takes on someone else's punishment for sin, but that does not mean he himself becomes sinful.

So, although it sounds like "hedging one's bets," it is probably true to say that Isaiah has a view of suffering that is not reducible to one theory. It is multifaceted and is effective in several different ways. This is somewhat like the case of New Testament understandings of the atonement accomplished by Jesus. Various images and ideas are used to express and "explain" his achievement, and one single theory cannot cover all aspects.

⸺

We should note one further remarkable idea in Isaiah's account of the role of the suffering servant of God. It is that the servant is given a new life by God even after his suffering and passing through death. The prophet says to God, "When you make his life an offering for sin he shall see his offspring and shall prolong his days . . . Out of his anguish he shall see light; he shall find satisfaction through his knowledge" (53:10–11).

This utterance is most unusual in the Old Testament, where the idea of an afterlife is not about light and satisfaction. It is more an experience of "*sheol*"—a shadowy, uncertain existence in a bleak underworld; life in the tomb. But here in Isaiah an emerging belief in an afterlife is expressed, in which God rewards the righteous sufferer and ensures that justice is finally done, and that the agonies of the sufferer are transformed into joy and peace.

The text of Isaiah 53:10–11, relating to an afterlife, is frustratingly brief, but has some similarities with phrases in Psalms 49:15 and 73:23–24. All of these affirmations seem to indicate a relationship with God, which is more than a ghostly existence in the shadowy world of death.

Surprisingly, if we go back to the first section of Isaiah to look at chapter 26 and verse 19, we read there:

> Your dead shall live,
> their corpses shall rise
> O dwellers in the dust,
> Awake and sing for joy!
> For your dew is a radiant dew,
> and the earth will give birth
> to those long dead.

This new hope is linked to the promise of new life after the years of oppression under an imperial power—in this case, Assyria. The context is that of the whole nation of Judah. Isaiah insists on the need for "a righteous nation"; and the note of hope is sounded after the desperate prayers from the people are poured out to God. Just prior to this passage in chapter 26, the people of God are pictured as writhing in something like the birth-pangs of a woman in labor, who "gave birth only to wind"; and the nation "won no victories on earth."(v. 18) But then, astonishingly, God raises the dead to life. This is a quite novel idea, especially if it comes from the original Isaiah, a prophet of the eighth century BC. There is no indication of a later insertion. So the concept of the afterlife, even in the early writings of the Old Testament, is complex and not black and white at all.

The Isaianic theology of both chapter 26 and 53 seems rather akin to Paul's idea (in 1 Cor 15:18) of resting and "falling asleep in the Lord" in the immediate aftermath of death, ready to rise again through God's power and mercy to something greater. Or perhaps it is like the hope of a renewed earth on which God's will is obeyed and the people live in peace and harmony. Romans 8:21 speaks of the physical creation being released from its bondage to decay at the same time as the dead are raised. This would then involve the redemption of the body (see Rev 20:4).

⁂

The suffering servant passages of Second Isaiah were certainly well known in the Early Church, and were applied to Jesus as Messiah. The passages were understood as messianic prophecies, which spoke clearly of the necessity of Jesus' own sufferings and of the purpose of those sufferings in terms of achieving for others a liberation from the power of sin and a new relationship with God. Matthew's gospel refers specifically to Isaiah 53:4 and quotes it (in Matt 8:17): "He took our infirmities and bore our diseases." Matthew takes up the idea of the suffering servant again in the Passion narrative (26:63). Paul also seems to allude to the servant songs in several places, and the idea is similar in each case: Jesus was being wounded for our rebellions or crushed for our guilt (see Isa 53:5 and compare with 2 Cor 5:21 and Rom 4:25). The first letter of Peter also seems to be aware of the servant songs, when the author writes (in 1 Pet 2:24), "he bore our sins in his body on the cross, so that, free from sins, we might live for righteousness; by his wounds you have been healed."

Thus, in the New Testament, the passages from Second Isaiah are not only understood as fulfilment of prophecy, but also as theological interpretations of Jesus' atoning death for sin. The Early Church developed theories of the atonement, not all of which are faithful to Isaiah's understanding of the servant's role, but which are certainly informed by Isaiah's writing. Today however we must be very careful to investigate and figure out the meaning of Isaiah's prophecies in the context of his own times, before we start to jump across the great chasm between those times and the life and death of Jesus in the first century AD, let alone try to bridge the greater chasm between the sixth century BC and the twenty first century AD.

Perhaps what we can say with some confidence is that the Servant Songs of Isaiah have influenced the New Testament and the Christian world ever since by demonstrating that suffering—even suffering leading to death—can, despite its negative impact, have a purpose and a positive effect on the lives of many people.

This, as we shall see, is the position taken up in the New Testament writings as a whole. Christ's own sufferings (and death) are regarded as having a positive impact and salvific effect upon the lives of those who have faith in him—both at the time of his earthly mission and ever since.

CHAPTER FIVE

THE PURPOSE OF SUFFERING IN THE NEW TESTAMENT

As we move from the Old Testament to the New, we experience a consistent and coherent understanding of suffering. Rather than being purely an affliction—and often an unjust one—suffering now seems to have a more positive purpose in life. But at the same time, suffering from the New Testament perspective, appears to be more narrowly defined. It does not consider all the bad things that unexpectedly happen to people. Rather, the central focus is on the suffering that comes as a result of living the Christian life. The New Testament authors are particularly interested in what Dennis Hamm calls "apostolic suffering . . . the suffering consequent upon pursuing a God-given mission."[1]

For the New Testament Christian, suffering is certainly not something to be actively sought—say, for mortification of the body or for spiritual discipline or anything like that—but rather it now appears to come uninvited as an inevitable and integral part of the spiritual life. The Christian of New Testament times, by becoming a Christian, begins to run the race of a godly life. Paul speaks of this "race of life" in Philippians 3: "forgetting what lies behind and straining forward to what lies ahead, I press on towards the goal for the prize of the heavenly call of God in Christ Jesus" (Phil 3:13–14).

It is a race that is like an obstacle race: exhausting, dangerous and the crowd watching it are sometimes hostile, throwing objects or tripping the Christian up. In spite of all this, Christians are encouraged to run their race and not to grow weary amidst adversity.

---

1. In Miller, *Suffering and the Christian Life*, 19.

In the letter to the Hebrews, chapter 11 is devoted to a roll call of those who have lived faithful lives. Then in chapter 12, the author comes to Jesus, who lived the exemplary life we should imitate: "Let us run with perseverance the race that is set before us, looking to Jesus the pioneer and perfecter of faith, who for the joy that was set before him endured the cross, despising the shame, and is seated at the right hand of the throne of God" (12:1b–3).

So the Christian life in the New Testament is far from being the place of protection and sanctuary we might imagine it to be: far from it, the call to the Christian life is a call to suffering—but paradoxically also a call to glory. For by enduring, persevering and finishing the race, the Christian inherits a reward—the crown of eternal life; far better than the crown of laurels given at the Olympic Games. As the Apostle Paul has it, "We suffer with Christ that we may also be glorified with him" (Rom 8:17). In writing to the Church at Philippi, Paul congratulates the congregation for accepting the suffering of the Christian life in the right spirit: God "has graciously granted you the privilege not only of believing in Christ, but of suffering for him as well—since you are having the same struggle that you saw *I* had, and now hear that I still have" (Phil 1:29).

In truth, the Apostle Paul seems rather to relish talking about his suffering. He regards it as the badge of honor he is able to wear because he is living the authentic Christian life. Paul challenges the Jewish "false teachers" at Corinth by showing how he is outdoing them in suffering for Christ:

> With far greater labors, far more imprisonments, countless floggings, often to the point of death. Five times I have received from the Jews the forty lashes, minus one. Three times I was beaten with rods, once I received a stoning. Three times I was ship-wrecked . . . in danger from rivers, danger from bandits, danger from my own people, danger from Gentiles, danger in the city, danger in the wilderness, danger at sea, danger from false brothers and sisters;in toil and hardship, through many a sleepless night, hungry and thirsty, often without food, cold and naked (2 Cor 11:23b–27).

Paul's life would clearly make an exciting action movie, but it would have to be X rated. And yet the worst aspect of all his sufferings he leaves to the end: "Besides all this, I am under daily pressure because of my anxiety for all the churches" (v. 28). Many of us who are or have been church leaders can sympathize with that!

Paul even goes so far as to say that he is completing the messianic sufferings lacking up until then. "I am now rejoicing in my sufferings for your sake, and in my flesh, I am completing what is lacking in Christ's afflictions for the sake of his body, that is, the Church" (Col 1:24). In saying this, Paul might sound either like a megalomaniac or a masochist, according to your point of view! If the first, then he is filled with hubris, comparing himself to Jesus Christ and speaking as though his sufferings were part of the atonement. If the second—a masochist—then he is inviting suffering by acting like an attention-seeking martyr. Yet, in truth, he is neither a megalomaniac nor a masochist. He is simply echoing the first century idea that in the last times there would be many woes to be endured by faithful believers. These were regarded as part of the suffering brought on by the opposition to God and to his Messiah.

In view of all this, we could now go on to say that Christians, according to the New Testament, are particularly likely to draw upon themselves the suffering that comes through *persecution*. The letter of 2 Timothy puts it bluntly: "Indeed, all who want to live a godly life in Christ Jesus will be persecuted" (2 Tim 3:12). The world's opposition to the gospel and to Christ's coming thus expresses itself in malice and even in violence towards believers in Christ. Why should this be? Part of the answer must be that the Christian is seen in the New Testament as a type of *the prophet*, and prophets of the Old Testament were invariably persecuted for their proclamation of "The Word of the Lord." Jeremiah knew what was coming when he was called, and tried to excuse himself: "Ah Lord God! But I do not know how to speak, for I am only very young" (Jer 1:6); and Isaiah similarly tried to avoid his call by giving a different excuse: "Woe is me . . . I am a man of unclean lips, and I live among a people of unclean lips" (Isa 6:5). In response, God had to make Jeremiah like "a fortified city, an iron pillar, and a bronze wall" (Jer 1:18), to protect him against his detractors and his persecutors. And Isaiah had his lips cleansed by having a burning coal placed on them! (Isa 6:6–7).

In the *New* Testament, Matthew makes the point clearly about the fate of those who speak prophetically: when Christians are reviled and persecuted and spoken against slanderously, it is because (and I quote) "in the same way they persecuted the prophets who were before you" (5:12).

Besides being like a prophet, the Christian of the New Testament is also identified with Christ, and his or her life is conformed to that of Christ. Thus, the suffering and persecution experienced by Jesus Christ is also, to a lesser extent, the lot or fate of his disciples. In Mark's gospel, Jesus speaks on three separate occasions about the suffering and death he must face as his destiny. In Mark 8:31, it tells us, "He began to teach them that the Son of Man must suffer greatly and be rejected by the elders, the chief priests and the scribes, and be killed, and rise again after three days." The Greek word for rejection here, "*apo-dokimasthenai*," means rejection after careful evaluation or assessment. In other words, the powers that be have examined

Jesus' claims, have observed his ministry and have dismissed both. After Jesus' observations about his own rejection, he goes on to speak about his followers: "If any want to become my disciples, let *them* deny themselves and take up *their* cross and follow me" (8:34).

In chapter 10 of Mark's gospel, Jesus makes this link between his own mission and that of the disciples even clearer. He tells the disciples that far from having a glorious life they are destined for humble service: "Whoever wishes to become great among you must be your servant, and whoever wishes to be first among you must be slave of all. For the Son of Man came not to be served but to serve, and to give his life as a ransom for many" (10:43–45). The *"mathetes"*—the disciple, or literally, "learner"—is not greater than the master, and models his or her life on that of the teacher.

The persecuting attitude from the world towards the believing community is also highlighted in *John's* gospel. Jesus himself warns his disciples "If the world hates you, be aware that it hated me before it hated you. If you belonged to the world, the world would love you as its own . . . If they persecuted me, they will persecute you" (John 15:18, 20). But Jesus' comments in John also have a *positive* twist and finish on a strangely encouraging note: "I have said this to you, so that in me you may have peace. In the world you will face persecution, but take courage, I have overcome the world" (16:33).

So there is a powerful paradox in New Testament teaching: suffering will come to you if you follow Christ openly, but nevertheless, you should rejoice and be glad, for your suffering is a sign that you are doing God's work and are being treated as Jesus was. For this reason, God will bless you. In this life, in the midst of troubles and afflictions, you will find peace, joy and fulfilment. Paul's letter to the Philippians, so eloquent about his sufferings, is the very place where Paul also speaks most about the joy experienced in the Christian life. In fact, the word "joy" or the equivalent verbal form is used 53 times in the letter.

⁓

It might be worth pausing for a moment to consider why Christianity in the United Kingdom *rarely* seems to be accompanied by suffering or by persecution. Is it because people in the western world—including Christians—do everything possible to avoid suffering, and regard it as an unmitigated disaster when it overtakes them? (We will consider this further in the next chapter). Or alternatively, is it because Christians in the west are NOT open about their faith and therefore do not incur much hostility from the world? In the latter case, there is too little difference between the church and the world; too little to make the world feel threatened in its ways. When there *is* a challenge to the ways of the world—to the level of poverty in our society, to the scandal of personal debt and the malpractice of loan sharks, to the immoral speculation of rich bankers gambling with our money—then there is often a sharp reaction. But perhaps we need more challenges from the church to the world in order to see authentic Christian suffering and persecution in the western church.

To conclude this point, let us remind ourselves of the words Jesus spoke in the Sermon on the Mount (Matt 5:10–11): "*Blessed* are you when people revile you and persecute you and utter all kinds of evil against you falsely on my account. Rejoice and be glad, for your reward is great in heaven." He goes on to say that believers are *the salt of the earth*; and in this context he is perhaps not speaking of salt as giving flavour, but of salt as having a stinging, painful effect on a wound, even though it is antiseptic and assists healing. On such an interpretation, the world has open wounds that should be "stung" and these "wounds" will be cauterized by the Christian witness. Perhaps this interpretation will sharpen up the Christian witness!

Finally, as a rider to all this, we must not forget that persecution is indeed rife in many parts of the modern world, even if *we* remain cushioned from most of it in the so-called "enlightened" western world. We only have to turn our attention to the Middle East, where Christianity has been on the defensive and in decline for some considerable time now. In the cradle of Christianity—in Syria, Iraq and Iran in particular, the faith is under great pressure, Christians are persecuted and Churches attacked.[2] There are also many other places where the words of the New Testament about suffering and persecution are an everyday reality—in Pakistan, in Egypt—and in Russia if you do not belong to the Orthodox Church. And the list goes on.

Thus, the New Testament has a lot to say about the suffering and persecution which are an inevitable part of the Christian life, but when it comes to *other people's suffering*, then the New Testament has a different approach entirely. The suffering of *Christians* is well documented in abstract statements and in exhortations about persevering and enduring through times of adversity. This is one of the key themes of the New Testament. However, *the metanarrative of the New Testament is the coming of the kingdom of God,* and this kingdom means, among other things, the overcoming of pain and distress and all kinds of suffering. Such things belong to the evil that is pitted against God's will. These things are to be opposed, pushed back and banished from this world as far as possible. The coming of the kingdom and the alleviation of suffering is not so much elucidated in abstract terms: it is demonstrated

---

2. Some of this is well documented in Dalrymple, *From the Holy Mountain*, but since the book's publication, matters have got much worse.

in action and shown in the narratives of Jesus' life and in the lives of his followers (especially in the book of *The Acts of the Apostles*).

Jesus himself is shown as constantly relieving suffering of all kinds—physical, mental and spiritual. In fact, we could go so far as to say that Mark's gospel has it that Jesus manifests the kingdom of God through his words and actions. He is *the embodiment* of the kingdom, and this is largely seen in his exorcisms (pushing back the boundaries of evil) and in his healings (bringing new life to those under the yoke of suffering and disability).

Mark's gospel has an enthusiastic comment on Jesus' work and ministry for the alleviation of suffering. In chapter 1 (vv. 32–34) we read:

> That evening, at sunset, they brought to him all who were sick or possessed with demons. And the whole city was gathered around the door. And he cured many who were sick of various diseases, and cast out many demons; and he would not permit the demons to speak, because they knew him.

In the gospels generally, Jesus also showed that this attitude of sympathy and compassion must be extended *to all people*, and not only to those within one's own faith community or those considered good enough. Great swathes of the gospel narratives—nearly a quarter—are dedicated to Jesus' healing miracles and exorcisms. There is no recorded case where he refused to help a person in need, be it a leper, a prostitute, a Roman soldier or any other foreigner. He has scant regard for the purity laws which would keep him from even speaking to certain outcast people, let alone conversing with them, touching them and healing them. The woman who was hemorrhaging for twelve years; and therefore utterly impure in the eyes of most Jews—the one who "stole" healing power from Jesus without asking his permission (Mark 5:25–34), even this woman was accepted and healed once Jesus had ascertained her identity. He even compliments her: "Daughter, your faith has made you well; go in peace and be healed of your disease." She is sent off with a blessing. Jesus shows himself truly to be "the man for others."

His concern and compassion are not only shown in healing many people of various illnesses, but also in offering help in cases of mental illness. The Gadarene demoniac seems to be an extreme case of this. At the outset, this Gentile is depicted wandering naked among the tombs of the dead, (anathema to the Jews), and was "always howling and bruising himself with stones" (Mark 5:5). By the end of the episode and after Jesus's exorcism, the man is seen "clothed and in his right mind" (5:15). Not only is he given peace of mind and a quiet spirit, but he is also restored to the community: "Go home to your friends," Jesus tells him. "Tell them how much the Lord has done for you, and what mercy he has shown you" (5:19).

Jesus is also shown on several occasions in the gospels giving spiritual counsel. We see this particularly in John's gospel, with Nicodemus in chapter 3 and the Samaritan woman at the well in chapter 4. Then later in the gospel, when Jesus heals the man born blind, he also assists him to have a real and open faith. Jesus asks him "Do you believe in the Son of Man?" The man responds, "Who is he, sir? Tell me, that I may believe in him," and Jesus then brings him out of fear and hesitation into a new life, by saying; "you have seen him, and the one speaking with you is he." Then the man says, "Lord, I believe," and he worships Jesus (John 9:35–38).

᠊᠊᠊᠊

Thus, because this is so central to the narrative flow of the NT it becomes clear that the central duty or task of a Christian in the New Testament is to *alleviate suffering*, to show compassion, to draw alongside the sufferer. In order to bring healing and wholeness into the world, Paul instructs the congregation in Rome: "Rejoice with those who rejoice, weep with those who weep" (Rom 12:15). A certain empathy is instilled through the apostle's teaching in order to ensure that those who suffer will be helped. Such a mindset has to be inculcated, so that Christians are always willing to serve and help those who are in difficulties. In Colossians 3:12 Paul sums up the right attitude when he says:

> As God's chosen ones, holy and beloved, clothe yourselves with compassion, kindness, meekness and patience. Bear with one another and, if anyone has a complaint against another, forgive each other.

Where compassion and fellow-feeling seem to have fallen away, Paul gives a stark warning in 1 Corinthians, in the context of the communion service: "All who eat and drink without discerning the body, eat and drink judgement against themselves. For this reason many of you are weak and ill and some have died" (11:29–30). Now what does "discerning" (*diakrinon*) the body" mean here? My understanding is that is means taking account of others in the Body of Christ and being attentive to their needs. Preparing for communion whilst being in bad relationships or whilst ignoring others who are being treated badly—these are serious offences for Paul the pastor. In the Corinthian church, it seems that the love-feast (agape meal) preceding the Eucharist had become a time when some ate far better food than others, and when some were left with nothing. Such a scenario is completely unacceptable to Paul.

And Paul is not only concerned about fellowship and loving relations among the believers in a particular community. He also sets himself the task of instilling into *all* his congregations an attitude of self-sacrifice and compassion towards those suffering *beyond* his own churches and beyond the church itself. His collection for those afflicted by a severe famine in Jerusalem seems to have been the great charitable project that Paul organized among all his people. It is mentioned in a number of his letters, beginning with Galatians, after Paul had been asked by the leaders in Jerusalem "to remember the poor" (Gal 2:10). Over two decades Paul takes this request very seriously, setting up a network for famine relief for those suffering in Judea (see also Acts 11:27–30). Paul's campaign starts on his second missionary journey. He refers to it in Galatians 6:6–10 and more pointedly in 1 Corinthians 16:1–4, where he exhorts the Christians to lay money aside each Sunday and to save whatever extra they earn, so that he, Paul, can take a sizeable gift to Jerusalem on his next visit. In the letter of 2 Corinthians, Paul devotes no less than two chapters (8—9) to the collection. We discover that the Macedonian churches have given very generously, despite their own poverty. Then Paul also writes to the Romans about the collection. There he sees the work as not only charitable famine relief, but also as a means of uniting Jew and Gentile in a single worthwhile mission project. He argues that "if Gentiles have shared in the Jews' spiritual blessings, they owe it to the Jews to share with them their material blessings" (Rom 15:27).

Some time later we learn from Acts 24 that Paul has been brought before governor Felix and there he tells Felix, "I came to bring my people gifts for the poor and to present offerings" (v. 17). Paul sees this gift as primarily for the relief of suffering, but also as a way of uniting his predominantly Gentile churches to the mother church in Jerusalem.

The whole project is regarded by Paul as a sacred mission, a mission of reconciliation, almost an act of worship to a God who approves this offering of generosity and kindness towards those who suffer. Thus, Paul's actions show that the relief of suffering warms the very heart of God.

⸻

Returning to the gospels, we can also discover some wisdom about the *cause* of suffering. When Jesus heals the man born blind, he is asked, "Rabbi, who sinned, this man or his parents, that he was born blind?" (9:20). He answered, "Neither this man nor his parents sinned; he was born blind so that God's work might be revealed in him" (v. 3). In this brief exchange, Jesus refutes the entire premise of the deuteronomic theology. These writings of the Old Testament, mentioned earlier, hold that a righteous man is rewarded with prosperity and long life, while a sinful man is punished and he and his children and his children's children have to suffer the consequences of his sin. It is true to say that often sin does lead to problems in life: bad choices and irresponsible behavior have consequences. However, Jesus is not willing to say that suffering is always a consequence of sin, nor does he allow a suffering person to be condemned or judged, as though they brought the suffering upon themselves.

The rather simplistic approach in parts of the Old Testament is also undermined in Luke's gospel, in chapter 13 (vv. 1–4), when Jesus is asked about some Galileans killed by Pilate when they made sacrifices, and about the eighteen people who were killed when the tower of Siloam collapsed and fell on them. Jesus made it abundantly clear that all of these people were no worse sinners than anyone else in Israel. He simply called the questioners to repentance and implicitly censured their judgemental, self-righteous attitude. "Do you think they were worse offenders than all the others? No, I tell you, unless you repent, you will all perish just as they did" (vv. 4–5). The suffering of people—even of those deemed to be "sinners"—is not a result of God's judgement, nor even of God's will, but a consequence of the risks attendant upon living in an imperfect world. Nobody is in a position to stand in judgement on others: suffering should evoke a response of compassion, not of condemnation.

Jesus also seems to distinguish between what *life* throws at us or afflicts us with, and what *God* intends for us. God's attitude—his true will—is highlighted by Jesus is the Sermon on the Mount: "He makes his sun rise on the evil and the good, and sends his rain on the righteous and the unrighteous" (Matt 5:45). In this life, God shows generosity and grace *to all*—life can be a blessing to those who are self-seeking as well as to those who are giving and loving. On the other hand, no one can be sure what "the slings and arrows of outrageous fortune" might throw at them.

Thus we see in all four gospels that Jesus's ministry is outward looking and that everything he does is for the benefit of others. He is always out in the world, active in alleviating suffering and assisting people towards physical, mental and spiritual health and wholeness. Clearly, he sees this as being the will of God. His approach is summed up in the words, "I did not come to be served but to serve and to give my life as a ransom for many" (Mark 10:45). He is constantly at work relieving the sufferings of other people, no matter whether they are poor or rich, young or old, Jew or Gentile, pure or impure in the sight of the Law.

And the apostle Paul teaches his congregations to have a similar attitude; what he calls the mindset of Christ (Phil 2:5). This means that the people must lay aside any longing for privileges, any desire for power. They must be content to act as servants or slaves of one another; always ready to help those in trouble or any who are suffering.

∽

Now if we briefly turn to The Acts of the Apostles, we see that, when the early church embarked upon its mission, the disciples of Jesus acted in exactly the same way as the master, healing and helping wherever there were cases of need. The work began with Peter's healing of the man lame from birth being carried into the Temple to continue with his customary begging at the Beautiful Gate (Acts 3:2 ff). Peter told the man that he had no silver or gold for him, and went on, "yet what I have I give you: in the name of Jesus Christ of Jesus Christ of Nazareth, stand up and walk" (v. 60). The man then went off, "walking and leaping and praising God" (v. 9). The crowd that gathered around gave Peter the pretext for a long sermon! (Be careful what you do when a preacher is watching!) A little later on in Acts we read, "Now, many signs and wonders were done among the people through the apostles" (5:12). "They even carried out the sick into the streets, and laid them on cots and mats, in order that Peter's shadow might fall on some as he came by. A great number of people would also gather from the towns around Jerusalem, bringing the sick and those tormented by unclean spirits, and they were all cured" (5:15–16).

Luke deliberately writes as though the healings and exorcisms of the apostles run parallel to those of Jesus himself. Their ministry and mission are in many ways similar to his, except that they are now deliberately reaching out beyond the confines of Israel and into the Gentile lands. Also, they are now preaching faith in Jesus, whereas Jesus himself preached about the coming of God's kingdom; that is, the power of God imposing God's rule in areas of life where sickness and evil had taken hold and had caused great suffering.

∽

So to sum up, the New Testament is very preoccupied with suffering; but it has two perspectives on the subject. The first is that suffering is incurred by Christians because they are living in a world hostile to God and to the life of faith; the second is that the suffering incurred by others must be met by Christians with an attitude of compassion and sympathy. Like the master himself, they must respond to suffering with words, prayers and actions which will alleviate the suffering of others, without distinction or preference, that is, whoever they may be.

∽

The third and final main perspective on suffering in the New Testament concerns the suffering of Jesus himself and how the New Testament writers understand his achievements through his suffering and death on the cross.

The Passion narratives take up a considerable section of each gospel, a full third of the total in the case of Mark. But Jesus' suffering does not *begin* with his tribulations in Jerusalem. Paul describes Jesus' giving up his power and prestige in Philippians 2. In a hymn-like poem, we read that Jesus, "though he was in the form of God . . . emptied himself, taking the form of a slave . . . He humbled himself and became obedient to the point of death" (2:6–8). This passage takes in the whole sweep of Jesus' mission, from the time of his descent into this world right through to the time of his vindication and glory at the right hand of God. But the essential fact of the first half of the poem is that Jesus allowed himself to be both a slave without rights and a victim without power. He placed himself at the mercy of others and relinquished control.

In the *early* stages of his ministry, this meant that he could be exhausted by the demands of others but worse, could be abused and undermined by a political and religious establishment intent on preserving their own power and prestige. Early on in Mark's gospel we read that Jesus rose early one morning to go to a deserted place to pray alone (Mark 1:35). But then "Simon and his companions hunted for him" (v. 36). When they found him, they announced, "Everyone is searching for you" (v. 37). Jesus was allowed no rest or respite. And Mark also makes it clear that as Jesus fame and popularity grew, so the suspicion and opposition grew simultaneously. As early as chapter 2, after the healing of the paralytic lowered through the roof, the scribes take exception to Jesus forgiving the man's sins: "This is blasphemy!" they say, "Who can forgive sins but God alone?" (2:7) And thereafter, as the mission progresses, so the hostility increases simultaneously.

When we come to the Passion narrative and Jesus' journey to Jerusalem to meet with his destiny, the gospel writers do not dwell on the gruesome details of Jesus' flogging or even his crucifixion. They focus much more on the shame and humiliation he had to endure. The mental suffering is seen as at least as terrible as the physical pain. This mental suffering is highlighted in the Garden of Gethsemane. Jesus tells his disciples, "I am deeply anguished, even to death" (14:34). He then threw himself to the ground and prayed that, if possible, this fate or doom might pass from him (v. 35). Then he said, "Abba, Father, for you all things are possible, remove this cup from me. Yet not what I want, but what you want" (v. 36). Jesus had to suffer all this alone, for, as Mark makes clear, his disciples could not even stay awake to pray for him.

Then before the trial, Jesus endured the betrayal by Judas and the denials of Peter. The Jewish people turned against him, and they called for the murderer Barabbas to be released instead of Jesus. When it came to the trial and flogging, Jesus also had to put up with mocking and spitting (15:16–20).

The humiliation is compounded by the fact that Jesus was crucified between two common bandits. And we read that those who passed by derided him, shaking their heads and calling out sarcastically, "If you could destroy the temple and rebuild it in three days, why don't you save yourself and come down from the cross? The chief priests and scribes also mocked him and said, "He saved others but he can't save himself" (15:31).

Then after all that, Jesus had to undergo the cruellest suffering of all—the loss of his sense of God's presence and protection. He cried out in anguish, "My God, my God, why have you forsaken me?" (15:34). Throughout all of the passion narrative, the focus of all three synoptic gospels is not so much upon Jesus' physical torture as upon his mental anguish—his humiliation, shame and vulnerability.

What was then achieved by his obedience and willingness to go through such suffering to the point of death? In Gethsemane he must have doubted his own belief in his mission. He must have wondered whether his work had ended in failure and his life ended in a pointless nothingness. That was his real agony and suffering. But the gospel writers are unanimous in declaring that out of this suffering and death came victory: victory over human sin and cruelty, victory over the powers of evil and victory over death. *The suffering of Jesus turned out to be the instrument of salvation.*

Without entering into theories and doctrines of atonement, we can say that the whole of the New Testament bears witness to the fact that Jesus' suffering and death are seen to have had an overarching purpose and a spectacular achievement.

Mark does not offer a theory on all this, but he does link the cross or crucifixion with discipleship. In chapter 9 verse 31 he has Jesus teach the necessity of his suffering and death and link it to final victory and vindication: "The Son of Man is to be betrayed into human hands and they will kill him, and three days after being killed, he will rise again." A little later again, in chapter 10 verse 45, Mark has Jesus say to the disciples, "For the Son of Man came not to be served, but to serve and to give up his life as a ransom for many." This seems to be a clear allusion to Isaiah 53, which has the assertion, "Surely he has borne our infirmities and carried our diseases; yet we accounted him stricken, struck down by God, and afflicted; yet he was wounded for our transgressions and crushed for our iniquities; upon him was the punishment that made us whole, and by his bruises we are healed" (Isa 53:4–5). Mark is crystal clear that there is a link between Jesus' suffering and our healing.

This section of 2nd Isaiah and other similar passages, known as the Servant Songs or poems of the suffering servant came to be regarded as relating to Jesus specifically right from the time of the earliest church.

Matthew makes this explicit by quoting from chapter 53 in 8:17. As a conclusion to Jesus's "casting out the evil spirits with a word, and curing all who were sick" (8:16), Matthew writes, "This was to fulfil what had been spoken through the prophet Isaiah, 'He took our infirmities and bore our diseases.'" Matthew clearly links Jesus' suffering and death with our healing and release from suffering. This is the great paradox of salvation.

The Apostle Paul uses a whole variety of metaphors and images to describe Jesus' achievement through his suffering and death, and the most central is the idea of Jesus being a sin offering or sacrifice for sin. This links to the Temple practice, where the High Priest on just one day of the year—the Day of Atonement—was allowed into the Holy of Holies in order to make the sacrifice of a bull and a goat on the altar, to atone for the sins of Israel and to seek God's forgiveness of the people's sins. The High Priest's sacrifice and prayer was regarded as effective, but the sacrifice had to be repeated every year and other sin offerings had to be made regularly in the Temple. Now, Paul sees Jesus' sacrifice as the one and only perfect and sufficient sacrifice good enough to attain forgiveness of sins *permanently*. There is no need for any further sacrifice after Jesus' perfect sacrifice. And through Jesus' work a new relationship could be forged between sinful human beings and God himself. Paul argues in Romans 3 (vv. 21–26) that all who have sinned are now justified and redeemed through Christ Jesus, "whom God put forward as a sacrifice of atonement by his blood, effective through faith" (v. 25). Thus, God treats those who have faith in Christ as forgiven through Christ's sacrifice on their behalf.

The writer to the Hebrews puts it somewhat differently. Jesus is the ideal High Priest seeking forgiveness of sins, but he himself is also the perfect sin offering: "When Christ had offered for all time a single sacrifice for sins, he sat down at the right hand of God ... For by a single offering, he has perfected for all time those who are now sanctified" (Heb 10:12–14). This argument about the efficaciousness of sacrifice is difficult for us in the 21st century to understand, but it is certainly central to New Testament thought.

Paul also has other ways of explaining Jesus' achievement. One of the most important of these is victory over the powers of evil. In Colossians 2:15 he writes, "He (Jesus) disarmed the rulers and authorities and made a public example of them, triumphing over them in it." This echoes the practice of the Roman emperors, who, in the wake of a victory over their enemies, would stage a grand procession through the triumphal arches leading into Rome, with groups of captives dragged along in the wake of the all-conquering Roman army.

But in the context of Colossians, Paul is writing about what he calls "the elemental spirits of the Universe" (v. 8). It is they who are now subject to the all-conquering Jesus Christ. They have been imprisoned and their powers taken away. They will now be subdued by the Holy Spirit for those who have faith in Christ's victory. Romans 8:37–39 seems to have a similar outlook when Paul writes that "neither death, nor life, nor angels, nor rulers, nor things to come, nor powers, nor height nor depth, nor anything in all creation will be able to separate us from the love of God in Christ Jesus."

For Paul, Jesus has achieved forgiveness of sins, the destruction of evil powers, liberation from slavery (which is the root meaning of "redemption"), and reconciliation—both to God and to one another. This latter theme (of reconciliation) takes up a considerable section of 2 Corinthians (especially 5:16–21). For Paul we are truly "a new creation" (5:17) through the achievement of Christ.

So the suffering of Jesus has an overriding purpose—to achieve for us a new life involving forgiveness of sin, a new closeness to God as our father, and a life liberated from the power of sin and the elemental powers of evil in the world.

In the light of Christ's purposeful suffering, the suffering of the Christian also has a purpose. We have already seen that one aspect of this is that the Christian draws closer to Christ through suffering. The Christian's suffering is a conforming to the life of Christ and, if endured courageously and with fortitude, will make the Christian more Christlike . . . Suffering can serve to educate us in maturity of faith, in wisdom, in strength of will, and in endurance.

Thus, suffering can build true Christian character, as it says in Romans 5:3–5: "We boast in our sufferings, knowing that suffering produces endurance, and endurance produces character, and character produces hope, and hope does not disappoint us, because God's love has been poured into our hearts through the Holy Spirit that has been given to us." Growth into maturity is actually assisted by suffering when it is met by the right response—that of perseverance, patience, courage and trust in God.

Secondly, as we have also seen, Christian suffering teaches empathy and compassion for others. Christians suffer with those who suffer, and rejoice with those who rejoice. This fellow feeling and sympathy teaches a caring and loving respect for all people, and a willingness to make sacrifices in order to help and serve those who are suffering.

One of the key points of the letter to the Hebrews is that Jesus, as the heavenly high priest, has become one with us and can sympathize with us in our sufferings, because he himself has known human weakness and the suffering human flesh is heir to. Hebrews first argues that Jesus understands the human condition, "Therefore, he has to become like his brothers and sisters in every respect, so that he might be a merciful and faithful high priest in the service of God . . . Because he himself was tested by what he suffered, he is able to help those who are being tested" (2:17–18). The writer then goes on to say, "Every high priest chosen from among mortals is put in charge of things pertaining to God on their behalf, to offer gifts and sacrifices for sins. He is able to deal gently with the ignorant and wayward, since he himself is subject to weakness" (Heb 5:1–2).

The import of this is that Jesus is like any high priest, that is, an ordinary human being, and therefore fully able to understand human vulnerability. Then the writer concludes his argument by saying: "Although he was [God's] son, he learned obedience through what he suffered, and, having been made perfect, became the source of eternal salvation for all who obey him." In this way, Jesus' humanity and in particular, his suffering as a human being (not just on the cross) has made him the high priest who sympathizes, draws close and ministers to his people and offers them hope even in and through their suffering. The salvation achieved by Jesus is thus intimately connected to his incarnation, his true humanity, and above all, to his suffering. It is through suffering, and not in spite of suffering, that salvation is gained.

⁂

Finally, it remains to be said, but briefly, that Christian suffering is lived out in the hope of a full release from suffering in the future—in an eschatological time of vindication and glory when we are transformed and when we inherit what Paul calls "a spiritual body" no longer subject to decay or the ravages of mortality (1 Cor 15). In Romans 8 v. 18 Paul says: "I consider that the sufferings of this present time are not worth comparing with the glory about to be revealed to us. For the whole creation waits with eager longing for the revealing of the children of God." Thus, Christians, according to Paul, "have the hope that creation itself will be set free from its bondage to decay and will obtain the freedom of the glory of the children of God" (v. 21).

Suffering and sin spoil the world: however, this life, our world, still offers a worthwhile and fulfilling life for most people: a life which can be filled with challenges, with loving relationships, with beauty and with worthwhile activities. It is the will of God that people find in their life "shalom"—that is peace of mind and heart, health and wholeness and the freedom which allows good choices and a fulfilled life. Even though that will is sometimes and in some ways thwarted, nevertheless God intends that at the end of history the conditions of life will be changed and the distortions and dislocations caused by sin and suffering will be banished for ever.

SECTION THREE

A SUFFERING WORLD—
MODERN RESPONSES

CHAPTER SIX

SETTING THE SCENE

As Europe came out of the High Middle Ages and into the thirteenth century onwards, the world of Christendom experienced a great change in sensitivity. Jesus had previously been depicted on the cross as a serene and commanding figure, Christ as the Judge and Ruler; "*Christos Pantokrator.*" If not that, then he was a somewhat distant and forlorn figure on the cross, rather detached from the worshipper and certainly different from the rest of us. But in the thirteenth century, Francis of Assisi (1182—1226) began a cult of devotion to the person of the suffering Christ. Towards the end of his life, and just before he received in his own body the "stigmata"—the wounds of the crucified Christ, he said these words: "O Lord, I beg of you two graces before I die; to experience in myself in all possible fullness the pains of Your cruel passion, and to feel the same love that made you sacrifice Yourself for us." Francis desired even more than mere empathy; he wanted to know from the inside the emotions and pains that Jesus himself underwent in his passion and crucifixion.

This change of perspective can also be clearly seen in Thomas a Kempis' classic writing, *The Imitation of Christ*, composed in Latin between 1418 and 1427. These meditations, arising from the monastic life, show a desire to sense and feel the sufferings of Christ in order that we may draw closer to God. In the section entitled "On close friendship with Jesus," a Kempis writes, "How unmoved and hard you are without Jesus; how foolish and empty if you desire anything but him . . . To be without Jesus is a bitter hell, but to be with him is sweet paradise."[1] The complete engagement of the emotional life in such devotion to the person of Jesus gave rise to a

---

1. Kempis, *The Imitation of Christ*, 94.

new movement, called the "*devotio moderna*," which emphasized Jesus's humanity and in particular his suffering as an ordinary mortal like us.

In our own times too, there has been a great change in sensitivity to suffering. Right up until the late nineteenth century, people used to regard public hangings as entertainment and would watch with more fascination than repulsion as some poor "struggler" jerked about on the end of a rope in his or her death throes. And in the late 19th and early 20th centuries, cockfighting and bare knuckle fighting were common sports. Caning, beating and other types of corporal punishment were commonplace both at home and in schools.

Today, most people recoil with revulsion before sight of such pain and suffering. In the 21st century most western European countries have banned outright all forms of capital punishment and some European countries have also banned corporal punishment, including parental discipline of children by smacking. There is a strong emotional reaction among most people of our times in the face of any kind of suffering, except perhaps when it is hidden away, like the ill-treatment of animals reared for food. We now try to teach our children to empathize with anyone suffering.

Theologian Jurgen Moltmann stated that suffering "is the open wound of life in this world."[2] More recently, Elizabeth Dreyer, writing in "Suffering in Christian Life and experience"[3] said that "Suffering is a staple of life, a part of what it means to be a human being." She goes on to say this: "In the end we don't have much control over it, although our 'medicalized culture of comfort' in the developed world works heroically to convince us otherwise."

It is true to say that suffering has been an ever-present fact of life in our times. The twentieth century in particular witnessed some of the worst suffering the world has ever known, with the trench warfare of 1914–18, so vividly portrayed on our television screens, the Nazi Holocaust and suffering of World War II, the Stalinist Soviet purges, the Japanese rape of Nanking, the atomic bomb on Hiroshima, the Chinese so-called Great Cultural Revolution, the Cambodian killing fields, the Rwandan genocide, and more recently, wars in Iraq and Afghanistan. The list could go on for a painfully long time . . . And all this, without mentioning abject poverty in many countries leading to malnutrition, sporadic famine, the creation of millions of refugees and widespread sickness and disease.

Lee Strobel, in his book *The Case for Faith*,[4] describing some of the suffering he had witnessed, ends with: "But nothing shocked me so much

---

2 Moltmann, *The Trinity and the Kingdom*, 49.

3. In Miller, *Suffering and the Christian Life*, 129.

4. Strobel, *The Case for Faith*, 27.

as my visit to the slums of Bombay, India. Lining both sides of the noisy, filthy congested streets, as far as the eye could see, were small cardboard and burlap shanties, situated right next to the road where buses and cars would spew their exhaust and soot. Naked children played in open sewage ditches that coursed through the area. People with missing limbs or bodies contorted by deformities sat passively in the dirt. Insects buzzed everywhere. It was a horrific scene, where ... people are born on the sidewalk, live their entire lives on the sidewalk, and die a premature death on the sidewalk."

What are our reactions in the early 21st century to such occurrences and to widespread poverty and sickness?

Firstly, the improvement of standards of health care and standards of living in the western world has not only inured us to much of the suffering elsewhere in the world but has also raised our expectations that there is always a cure—even a panacea—for any unwanted suffering. Advertising bombards us with persuasive arguments about how drugs and surgery, creams, cosmetic surgery, stimulants, alternative medicines can alleviate all but the worst of our illnesses and suffering. Science and wealth have made it possible in most instances to ease pain, increase creature comforts, enhance health and postpone death.

Secondly, the communications revolution has raised our awareness of suffering. The news brings into our living rooms each day victims of war, natural disaster, starvation and disease on every continent. We are no longer ignorant of the plight of other people in distant foreign parts. We would at other times in history have had no knowledge of such suffering. But paradoxically, this knowledge can deaden our conscience at times and harden us to the pain of other people. Our constant exposure to troubles and grief in the media has made it more difficult to develop true empathy in the face of human misery.

Nevertheless, as I said, we have been sensitized to pain and suffering as never before. Through listening skills, through pastoral care, through sympathy for others in a plight we know we could have to undergo, we have learnt to share burdens, assist those grieving or struggling, alleviate pain and put ourselves in the shoes of others. As Pamela Cooper-White says, "Suffering is the starting point for all pastoral and practical theology."[5]

⇁

In addition to the causes and types of suffering that we have already considered, we should also make a distinction between suffering that we choose and suffering that befalls us uninvited. Ascetic practices like fasting and

---

5. In *The Wiley Blackwell Companion to Practical Theology*, 23.

praying have long been an important part of the Christian tradition. In more recent times, tremendous feats of endurance and even pain have been undertaken in order to raise money for charity. Recent examples might be the efforts of Sport Relief devotees: Davina McCall cycling, swimming and running in dire weather conditions from Edinburgh to London, and Alex Jones of the One Show undertaking an extreme perpendicular mountain climb in Utah, USA. Many have voluntarily embraced suffering to help others—donating an organ, risking life and limb in a rescue attempt, taking on a prophetic Christian leadership in the face of persecution and so on.

But then there is the suffering that comes to us unawares, and this is usually what causes the most distress. Daily life can throw up unexpected changes, and sometimes trials and tribulations: for example, unemployment, losing one's home, broken relationships, falling into debt, inner hurt from a cruel word, illness and health problems, being victim of an accident or an assault, and, in old age, the breakdown of sight, hearing, joints and mental abilities. All these things are hard to bear and raise many questions in people's minds about whether God cares, or whether there is a God to care.

There is also another distinction to make, and it involves our *response* to suffering. We can be surprised by sickness, disability or some other affliction and think to ourselves, "Why me? Why has this happened? It is not fair." On the other hand, we can accept that suffering is a fact of life and try to face it stoically or even positively when it comes our way. Aristotle, back in the c5th BC wrote: "Suffering becomes beautiful when anyone bears great calamities with cheerfulness, not through insensibility, but through greatness of mind."

On the other hand, faced with some kinds of suffering, we might say, not "Why me?" but instead, "Why not me?" or, "So many others have had to suffer." This might free us to think that we can feasibly turn our own suffering to positive effect rather than simply resenting it and sinking into self-pity. As Helen Keller, the famous deaf and blind writer once said; "Character can be developed in ease and quiet. Only through experience of trial and suffering can the soul be strengthened, ambition inspired and success achieved." She also said, "The whole world is full of suffering. It is also full of overcoming." The great civil rights activist, Martin Luther King, asserted that "human progress is neither automatic nor inevitable . . . Every step towards the goal of justice requires sacrifice, suffering and struggle; the tireless and passionate concern of dedicated individuals." Both Helen Keller and Martin Luther King were well acquainted with the reality of suffering; both were qualified to make these positive assertions.

The Nigerian British writer, Ben Okri, summed up this more positive response or frame of mind when he wrote, "The most authentic thing about us is our capacity to create, to overcome, to endure, to transform, to love and to be greater than our suffering." He regards suffering as the great challenge of life: what we make of it shows what kind of being we are.

Perhaps it requires not just strength of character to have a positive attitude, but also the recognition that life is a mixed bag: day to day we experience progress and setbacks, steps forward and knocks back, ups and downs. But that is not to say that *God* is to be confused with *life*. Just as we can stand above our suffering in some way, so God too stoops down to sympathize with us in our suffering and to draw alongside us. He does not will our suffering just as he does not will any evil, but what he *allows* is to be distinguished from what he desires. And in truth, sometimes it is only through suffering that God's purposes can come about. Many people have come to God through illness or through being laid aside from everyday activities. In his biography, Walter Maier argued that for a believer, pain and suffering can act as "one of the Father's ways of speaking to you; it is the evidence of his limitless love by which he would draw you further from evil and closer to him; the divine remedy which can cure you of pride and help you to lean more trustingly on the Lord."

Some would find this attitude far too complacent and simplistic. Surely much suffering merely grinds a person down, crushes the human spirit and saps our natural resilience. That is true, but on the other hand, it is also true that self-sufficiency and a desire to control life are the great sins of secular people in the 21st century. Thus, to relinquish control, to recognize that we are not truly self-sufficient and independent, is a lesson worth learning that can—given the right attitude—lead to new insights and new acceptance of God's sympathy and help. Sometimes the lesson that we are contingent creatures *not* always in control of our lives can only be learnt through suffering.

In this context the underrated virtue of *hope* also comes into its own. If we return to Martin Luther King again, he once said: "We must accept finite disappointment, but we must never lose infinite hope." The French poet and political writer Charles Peguy, in his prose poem, *Mystery of the Second Virtue,* painted a vivid picture of two fine ladies walking out with a little girl running ahead of them. The little girl was looking at everything eagerly and enthusiastically and reporting back to the matriarchs. Those "grandes dames" represented love and faith; the little girl represented hope.

Chapter 7

TWO WRITERS ON SUFFERING— C.S. LEWIS AND PHILIP YANCEY

C.S. Lewis

NOW IT SEEMS TO me that there are two main ways of looking at the problem of suffering today. There is a philosophical way—which I characterize as looking from the outside; and there is the personal way—which I characterize as looking from the inside. Interestingly, the great Christian apologist of the twentieth century, C.S. Lewis, wrote two books on suffering, and each is from one of these perspectives. The books are thus a fascinating contrast. The first—the philosophical investigation, entitled *The Problem of Pain* (1940), looks at suffering "from the outside"—from a detached, abstract point of view. The second, *A Grief Observed*, (1961) arises from Lewis' very personal experience of losing his wife Joy, after a relatively short marriage. These two responses to suffering, in general terms, constitute the most common responses in the modern age, and are worth examining.

The philosophical approach to suffering arises out of the age-old conundrum about a God of love who is all-powerful and who nevertheless allows suffering and evil to do great harm in the world. Back in the ancient Greek civilization, the philosopher Epicurus put the case this way: "Either God wants to abolish evil, and cannot; or he can, but does not want to; or he cannot and does want to. If he wants to, but cannot, he is impotent. If he can, but does not want to, he is wicked. So if God both can and wants to abolish evil, then how does evil come into the world?"

Looking at life from this point of view, many atheists regard the existence of suffering and evil in the world as incompatible with the existence of a good and beneficent God. In fact, Hans Kung, the Christian apologist, has called this problem of evil and suffering "the rock of atheism."[1] The problem is also neatly encapsulated by the modern philosopher H.J McCloskey, "Evil is a problem for the theist, in that a contradiction is involved in the fact of evil on the one hand, and belief in the omnipotence and omniscience of God on the other."[2] McCloskey, like many modern atheists regards belief in a good and loving God as irrational and illogical, given that suffering and evil are seen to run amok in the world.

Yet to say that "God exists" and "Evil and suffering exist" is not a logical contradiction if an explanation can be given as to why God thinks there is a sufficient reason to allow evil and suffering to exist—at least for the time being. God might have reasons for *not* automatically wanting to eliminate suffering and evil from the world. This is the case C.S. Lewis makes in *The Problem of Pain*. Lewis does not however begin by trying to answer the problem as we have just posed it: first he takes us a step back and asks a prior question: If pain and suffering make it impossible to believe in a good God, then why have all civilizations had a belief? He answers this question by arguing that most people have a sense of the numinous—of a spirit realm permeating, but going beyond, everyday reality. He thinks that at times in life most people are aware of an unseen presence or of awe in the face of some aspect of creation. Lewis also adds that humans have a built-in moral sense, and conceive of a God who has set the moral law of good and evil into the fabric of life.

Lewis then goes on to say that human choice depends upon free will and that free will requires a stable world rather than one in which God keeps intervening when things get rough or tough. God is not a grandfather who habitually indulges his children, Lewis asserts.[3]

Lewis's argument about freedom of the will has three main aspects. First, Lewis contends that the granting of free will to created beings like angels and human beings leads to a higher good than a world without any evil. To have free will implies having the freedom to make *bad* choices with evil consequences; choices which might well cause suffering. This cannot be the case if there is only one—good—choice.

Secondly, Lewis holds that life is good and—on balance—well worth living, despite the evil and suffering in it. In fact, a world where suffering

---

1. Kung, *On Being a Christian*, 432.
2. McCloskey, "God and Evil," 97.
3. Lewis, *The Problem of Pain*, 28.

and evil are allowed, enables a world where courage, endurance, nobility of spirit, compassion and caring, all become possible and attainable. In other words, the world is adapted for character formation and development. Adversity and suffering are the refining fires of human growth.

Thirdly, Lewis argues, God knows about our suffering and sympathizes with us, giving support and succor when people open their hearts to God's love, and enabling some good to come out of the suffering. God suffers with us, and also works through us so that "all things work together for good for those who love God" (Rom 8:28).

To return to the first argument—that of free will leading to a higher good than a world without any evil—Lewis attempts to answer this in his book, *Mere Christianity*.[4] The question he tackles there is: why did God create human beings with free will if he knew that they would upset and mess up his plans through immoral and selfish choices? Lewis writes in response:

> Why then did God give them free will? Because free will, though it makes evil possible, is also the only thing that makes possible any love or goodness or joy worth having. A world of automata—of creatures that worked like machines—would hardly be worth creating. The happiness which God designs for his higher creatures is the happiness of being freely, voluntarily united to Him and to each other . . . And for that, they must be free. Of course, God knew what would happen if they used their freedom the wrong way: apparently He thought it was worth the risk.[5]

Lewis estimates that some four fifths of the world's suffering is attributable to humankind's sin and cruelty: "It is men not God," he says, "who have produced racks, whips, prisons, slavery, guns, bayonets and bombs." And he goes on, "It is by human avarice or stupidity, not by the churlishness of nature, that we have poverty and overwork."[6]

Yet, despite the terrible effects of freedom of choice and free will in human history, Lewis contends that this gift creates a higher order of creation than a world where humans automatically follow the will of God.

The second argument follows from the first. In it, Lewis argues that a world with freedom of choice leads to noble qualities absent from a world without free will. Freedom allows for character formation and growth in maturity. He gives the example of an artist: the artist can knock off a sketch to amuse a child without much effort; but the masterpiece of his life—a

---

4. Lewis, *Mere Christianity*, 52.
5. Ibid.
6. *The Problem of Pain*, 77.

work upon which he expends great effort and much love—that work takes endless trouble. The artist actually suffers a good deal to bring the picture to perfection, but all this effort is far more worthwhile than the quick sketch done painlessly.[7]

Later in the book, Lewis writes these words about the formative effect of suffering: "I have seen great beauty of spirit in some who were great sufferers. I have seen men (*sic*) for the most part grow better, not worse, with advancing years, and I have seen the last illness produce treasures of fortitude and meekness from the most unpromising subjects.... If the world is indeed a 'vale of soul-making' it seems on the whole to be doing its work."[8]

In the book's concluding paragraphs, Lewis again returns to this theme, but adds something important—the pain of mental suffering. "Mental pain is less dramatic than physical pain, but it is more common and also more hard to bear. The frequent attempt to conceal mental pain increases the burden. It is easier to say, 'My tooth is hurting' than to say 'My heart is broken.'"[9]

⁓

Every one of us who has had children and seen them suffer as they become independent; trying to get through University or trying to get a good job or going through the pain of finding love in a partner and then losing it—every one of us knows that the mental pain that we experience at these times is worse than a physical illness.

Lewis then goes on to say; "Yet if the cause is accepted and faced, the conflict will strengthen and purify the character and in time the pain will usually pass. Sometimes, however, it persists and the effect is devastating; if the cause is not faced or not recognized, it produces the dreary state of the chronic neurotic. But some by heroism overcome even chronic mental pain. They often produce brilliant work and strengthen, harden, and sharpen their characters till they become like tempered steel."[10]

The third argument is that through suffering God draws close to us and sympathizes with us, helps us and accompanies us through our troubles. There are many people who imagine that God is one who is remote, on high, telling us what to do and having little to do with our daily woes and trials. But the Christian view—and Lewis's—is that God loves us and takes an interest in each one of us, creating us as unique individuals. Then Jesus, as revealer of God and as divine himself, shows beyond doubt that God is concerned to alleviate our suffering and sympathizes with our weakness and

7. Ibid., 30–31.
8. Ibid., 96.
9. Ibid.
10. Ibid., 144.

vulnerability. Lewis does not state this argument strongly in *The Problem of Pain* but it is implied and hinted at in many places.

Finally, there is a fourth argument in the book, which is somewhat distinct from the other three. It takes the form of regarding pain and suffering as a means of overcoming the endemic human problem of sin and rebellion against God.

Christians are by no means exempt from the problem of sin and cruelty which brings about so much suffering. Lewis enjoins Christians to take self-will seriously as an the underlying problem of human nature. Christians should recognize it and address it in themselves: as he writes; "Hence the necessity to die daily: however often we think we have broken the rebellious self, we shall still find it alive."[11] He regards this self-will as being active from a very young age, if not from birth: "We all remember this self-will as it was in childhood; the bitter, prolonged rage at every thwarting, the burst of passionate tears, the black Satanic wish to kill or die rather than to give in."[12]

Yet pain and suffering, while often being a consequence of sin and self-will, are also, curiously, part of the solution. When we ourselves have to suffer, our own pain and suffering can have the effect of awakening our conscience and our sense of sin: "God whispers to us in our pleasures, speaks in our conscience, but shouts in our pains; it is His megaphone to rouse a deaf world."[13] When things are going well with us, we become complacent, but when we face adversity or suffering, we are provoked to think more deeply about life. Thus, pain can have a beneficial effect in the long run. As Lewis puts it; "The full acting out of the self's surrender to God therefore demands pain."[14]

This is not all bad news, however, because "if pain sometimes shatters the creature's false self-sufficiency," nevertheless, in coming to God and in seeking help, the creature finds "that strength, and that alone, which God confers on him through his subjected will. Human will becomes truly creative and truly our own when it is wholly God's, and this is one of the many senses in which he that loses his soul shall find it."[15]

Thus suffering, in Lewis's view, serves to remind us that all the world's goods "were never intended to possess my heart, that my true good is in another world and my only real treasure is Christ. And perhaps, by God's grace, I succeed, and for a day or two become a creature consciously dependent

---

11. Ibid., 80.
12. Ibid., 79.
13. Ibid., 81.
14. Ibid., 87.
15. Ibid., 90.

upon God and drawing its strength from the right sources."[16] Lewis goes on to say that in this life we long for "settled happiness and security" but we can only find temporary and short-lived "joy, pleasure and merriment"—good in themselves, but leaving us longing for more. "We are never safe, but we have plenty of fun and some ecstasy." So we have to content ourselves with "a few moments of happy love, a landscape, a symphony, a merry meeting with our friends, a bathe or a football match."[17] We only find our true destiny beyond this life in the life to come.

To conclude our investigation of *The Problem of Pain*, we can end by saying that Lewis sees a paradox at the heart of suffering. The paradox is that suffering—despite its basic evil—can have certain good effects, if responded to with courage and humility. At the same time, suffering must always be alleviated wherever it is seen—and that applies to the suffering caused by pain and poverty equally. Jesus himself demonstrated this paradox in his own life. He knew in advance that his suffering and death was the will of God, and that it would bring about the great good of the healing and salvation of many. Yet at the same time, Jesus brought to Gethsemane a strong will to escape from suffering and death—"If it be possible, let this cup pass from me. But your will and not mine be done."

Now let us move on to Lewis's later short book, *A Grief Observed,* in which he looks at suffering "from the inside," from personal experience of pain and loss. He seemed almost to anticipate this book in the earlier *Problem of Pain* when he wrote: "All arguments in justification of suffering provoke bitter resentment against the author. You would like to know how I behave when I am experiencing pain, not writing books about it."[18] Fortunately, we do discover exactly how Lewis behaves when he experiences real pain and suffering, in his later offering, *A Grief Observed,* written in 1961, twenty one years after *The Problem of Pain*.

In 1956 Lewis married Joy Davidson, an American poet and academic who had two small children from a previous marriage. After four intensely happy years, Joy died of cancer and Lewis found himself alone again and inconsolable. Whilst going through an acute grieving process, Lewis wrote "notes" on his feelings and thoughts, which were later published as *A Grief Observed*. Author Penelope Fitzgerald considered this to be "the most touching and immediate of all Lewis's books."[19] The style of it is very dif-

---

16. Ibid., 94.
17. Ibid., 103.
18. Lewis, *The Problem of Pain*, 93.
19. Lewis, *A Grief Observed*. Quoted here in Faber & Faber edition of 2013. Fitzgerald is quoted from the back cover.

ferent from *The Problem of Pain*. Now Lewis's writing is filled with vivid imagery and personal detail. He dissects his moods and emotions, as well as his thoughts and insights.

The first reaction Lewis has to grief is that it resembles "fear." "The sensation is like being afraid. The same fluttering in the stomach, the same restlessness, the yawning. I keep on swallowing."[20] He also likens his first reactions to "being mildly drunk or concussed. There is a sort of invisible blanket between the world and me."[21] He tries to reflect and think clearly: "Love is not the whole of a man's life. I was happy before I ever met Joy."[22] But reason is of no assistance: "a sudden jab of red-hot memory and all this 'commonsense' vanishes like an ant in the mouth of a furnace."[23] He realizes a little later that his plight is made worse by too much thinking: "grief is compounded by the fact that you don't merely suffer, but have to keep on thinking about the fact that you suffer."[24] Lewis loses interest in the everyday routines of life, like shaving, bathing, keeping up appearances.

Then the big question rears its head: Where is God? With his unquiet mind and restless spirit, Lewis can find no consolation: "Go to him when your need is desperate . . . what do you find? A door slammed in your face, and a sound of bolting and double-bolting on the inside."[25] Where he normally finds God, now "there are no lights in the windows. It might be an empty house."[26] Lewis sounds a little like Job, as he complains, "Why is he so present a commander in our time of prosperity and so very absent a help in time of need?"[27] Lewis then remembers the death of a friend, and how at the time he felt certain about his continued life; even his enhanced life [after death]. But he has no such assurance about his wife, Joy.

He finds he can't easily talk to anyone to share the pain. The children look embarrassed and change the subject, "as if I were committing an indecency."[28] In fact, he feels that he is an embarrassment to everyone he meets: "to some I'm worse than an embarrassment. I am a death's head."[29] This highlights the fact that much suffering—and especially mental anguish,

20. Lewis, *A Grief Observed*, 5.
21. Ibid.
22. Ibid.
23. Ibid., 6.
24. Ibid., 10.
25. Ibid., 7.
26. Ibid.
27. Ibid., 8.
28. Ibid., 10.
29. Ibid., 11.

anxiety, depression and forms of mental illness, have to be endured alone. Other people do not understand; neither do they show much sympathy.

Then as time goes on a little, Lewis realizes that Joy was near death and when all hope was lost, they still had some happiness and gaiety.[30] This makes him understand that while thinking pulls much suffering into one mass, in fact "you don't meet a nameless horror, only each hour or moment that comes. All manner of ups and downs."[31] He also recognizes that he could never share Joy's suffering fully—"I had my miseries, not hers; she had hers not mine."[32] The mind can sympathize, but someone else can't know exactly what the sufferer feels.

Lewis has little time for the common sentimental takes on bereavement. He quotes the people who say that death is nothing. It doesn't matter.[33] Then there is what he calls "another piece of cant: she will live forever in my memory."[34] Such sentimental thoughts Lewis dismisses: "That's exactly what she won't do."[35] Lewis also has no time for the pious observation "She is now with God."[36] He goes on: "They tell me [Joy] is happy now, they tell me she is at peace. What makes them so sure?"[37] And yet he remembers that Joy's last words were, "I am at peace with God."

At this early stage of grief, Lewis is worried that he can't bring a clear picture of Joy up in his imagination. Nor does he have any very good photos to gaze at. He also can't pray to her or for her: "Bewilderment and amazement come over me. I have a ghastly sense of unreality, of speaking into a vacuum about a nonentity."[38] Yet his heart and body are still crying out, "Come back, come back."[39]

Moving on in time again, Lewis begins to be surprised that little commonplace things suddenly bring back a vivid memory: "The jokes, the drinks, the arguments, the lovemaking, the tiny, heartbreaking commonplaces."[40]

There is still a divorce between rational beliefs and feelings: "Talk to me about the truth of religion and I'll listen gladly. Talk to me about the duty

---

30. Ibid., 13.
31. Ibid.
32. Ibid.
33. Ibid., 15.
34. Ibid., 18–19.
35. Ibid., 19.
36. Ibid., 22.
37. Ibid., 24.
38. Ibid., 20.
39. Ibid., 22.
40. Ibid.

of religion and I'll listen submissively. But don't come talking to me about the consolations of religion or I shall suspect you don't understand."[41] This disjunction is also reminiscent of Job in his grieving, when he is willing to discuss matters but finds his "comforters" of no help at all. Yet Lewis is now beginning to realize that his anger vented at God and his doubts are coming from distress rather than reason. After doubting God's goodness, he then says, "I wrote that last night. It was a yell rather than a thought."[42] Again he abandons trying to think things through. His reasoning brings no comfort. "There is nothing we can do with suffering except to suffer it."[43]

Then at a later stage again, Lewis finds that he is not constantly returning to painful thoughts about Joy. Everything is still very flat, the atmosphere is "deadly,"[44] but he is entering a new phase, where Joy can suddenly seem vivid to him again, most especially when he is *not* anguished and tormented by grief. When he mourns her less, he remembers her best. Now in a calmer mood, he reflects that a lot of his earlier faith has been like "a house of cards."[45] He has had to go through this experience in order to knock it down—to rid himself of false ideas, such as that God is testing him or doing an experiment on his faith.

He then considers his earlier grieving: "I have gradually come to feel that the door is no longer shut and bolted. Was it my own frantic need that slammed it in my face?."[46] He compares himself to "the drowning man who can't be helped because he clutches and grabs."[47] He has not been knocking at heaven's door, but "hammering and kicking the door like a maniac."[48]

Once Lewis stops fretting about losing his vivid memories of Joy, to his surprise, he finds he now remembers her better: "She seems to meet me everywhere . . . a sort of unobtrusive but massive sense that she is, just as much as ever, a fact to be taken into account."[49] He then understands that "you don't get over it." The new reality lives on with you: "You can't forget it or

---

41. Ibid., 23.
42. Ibid., 27.
43. Ibid., 29.
44. Ibid., 31.
45. Ibid., 34–36.
46. Ibid., 40.
47. Ibid.
48. Ibid.
49. Ibid., 44.

get beyond it."⁵⁰ However, you can come to terms with it, make an accommodation: "There's no denying," says Lewis, "in some sense, I feel better."⁵¹

He now believes that his marriage "lives on" in some sense. He must not wallow too much in the aching and pain: "the less of them the better; so long as the marriage is preserved."⁵² He decides that "passionate grief does not link us to the dead, but cuts us off from them."⁵³ When he feels less sorrow, then Joy often "rushes into [his] mind in her full reality, her otherness."⁵⁴ He comes to see sorrow not as a state, but as a process: "Grief is a long valley where any bend may reveal a totally new landscape." "There is something new to be chronicled each day."⁵⁵ Now his familiar walks with Joy bring something different: "every horizon, every stile or clump of trees, summoned me into a past kind of happiness."⁵⁶

Lewis's thoughts turn to God again. He tells himself that "the five senses, an incurably abstract intellect, a haphazardly selective memory, a set of preconceptions and assumptions," cannot let in all of reality: "How much of total reality can such an apparatus let through?"⁵⁷ He finds at this stage that praise can be helpful to him. "By praising [God], I can still, in some degree enjoy her, and already, in some degree, enjoy Him."⁵⁸

He returns to the image of faith as a "house of cards." He has a horror of building a house of cards out of our reason or imagination—an idol that God will knock down. "The Real lies beyond that."⁵⁹ He adds, "Not my idea of God but God. Not my idea of Joy but Joy."⁶⁰

He muses on whether he can be reunited with Joy. At an early stage of grief he had dismissed the idea of "family reunions," as he put it. But now he asks the question of God, and feels that the answer is "a silent, certainly not uncompassionate gaze." God waives the question with "Peace, child, you do

50. Ibid., 45–46.
51. Ibid., 46.
52. Ibid., 47.
53. Ibid.
54. Ibid.
55. Ibid., 50.
56. Ibid., 51.
57. Ibid., 54.
58. Ibid., 53.
59. Ibid., 56.
60. Ibid.

not understand."[61] Lewis finds this reassuring. He now sees life not as God's great experiment, but as God's great enterprise.[62]

Finally, and very near the end of the book, Lewis has a vivid experience of Joy's presence—of her mind meeting his: "not a rapturous reunion of lovers—more like a telephone call,"[63] he says matter-of-factly. Yet it was "an extreme and cheerful intimacy." It is on this note that the book draws to a close.

Clearly, in *A Grief Observed* Lewis passed through several stages of grief. Elisabeth Kubler-Ross, in her well-known book of 1969, *On Death and Dying*, proposed five stages of the grieving process. People might experience them in order, but earlier stages can recur and the stages are not always so clear-cut as the analysis suggests. The stages are: Denial; Isolation; Anger; Bargaining ("if only . . ."—accompanied by a desire to regain control); Depression; and finally, Acceptance.

C.S. Lewis does seem to go through at least some of these stages, although he does not mention "bargaining." Certainly, isolation and numbness begin the process with him, then anger of the Psalmist's kind; a yell of pain at God. We also have the flatness of depression and finally, acceptance; although I would prefer to call this "coming to terms with a new reality" in Lewis's case. His faith affects his reactions a great deal, and Kubler-Ross does not take enough account of the fact that, with a person of faith, the final stage might be something positive, not mere acceptance. In Lewis's case, there is the sense that his wife, Joy, is at peace and in a new life with God: a life that he can sense, but not understand. He has hope that he will go into an enhanced state of being himself after death, and will perhaps know Joy again. This makes a huge difference to his grieving and sense of bereavement, once he gets past the earlier stages.

Philip Yancey

Now let us turn to another great Christian apologist on suffering; Philip Yancey, whose book *Where is God when it hurts* (1977) has become a bestseller on the subject. Yet, perhaps feeling that an update was necessary, Yancey much later wrote another popular book on the subject, *The Question that never goes away* (2013).

---

61. Ibid., 58.
62. Ibid., 61.
63. Ibid.

The first book was written when Yancey was only twenty-seven.[64] It has some echoes of C.S. Lewis's *The Problem of Pain*, but concentrates much more on personal interviews and visits, quotations and anecdotes to convey its argument and message. This makes the book full of human interest—most moving in parts—but extends its length considerably.

The first section is also rather different from Lewis's book, focussing on pain, not as a cause of suffering, but as a finely tuned and delicately calibrated early warning system. This network of pain sensors "reveals a marvellous design that serves our bodies well . . . Without pain, our lives would be fraught with danger, and devoid of many basic pleasures."[65] Yancey examines in some detail the lives of those suffering from leprosy and concludes that most of the effects of the disease—missing fingers and toes, damaged skin, etc.—have come about because the pain sensors have been numbed, making sufferers much more prone to injuring themselves.

The internal organs, Yancey asserts, only register pain when they need to. They are hidden away and are protected by the outer defences of the skin. Once something harmful gets past these defences, they usually fail to warn us of any discomfort or hurt: so "you could burn the stomach with a match, insert a needle through the lung, cut through the brain with a knife, crush the kidney in a vice, or bore through bone."[66] However, when pain needs to be signalled to the suffering victim, as in the case of stomach ache or appendicitis, then sensors are in place to give a warning. Yancey much admires the system by which internal organs are able to "refer" pain to the outer parts of the body, so that, for instance, heart attack victims "notice a burning or constricting feeling in the neck, chest, jaw or left arm"[67]; or again, if a very cold ice cream is consumed too fast, the stomach causes a headache to strike just behind the eyes!

Thus, the body's pain sensors are finely calibrated and are very sensitive; being designed to cause enough shock to the system to prevent us from damaging ourselves too much. It is when the pain network goes wrong that real problems arise. The same nervous system which inspires admiration and awe in a bio-engineer, can be the one which causes unwanted and even unnecessary suffering in its victim. As Yancey admits ruefully, "What about the side effects of pain as it grinds down the soul towards despair and

---

64. Yancey, *Where is God When it Hurts?* Quoted here (as *Where is God?*) in the second edition of 1990.

65. Yancey, *The Question that Never Goes Away*, 33–34.

66. Ibid., 32.

67. Ibid., 33.

hopelessness? Why the caprice of some lives tormented by arthritis, cancer or birth defects, while others escape un-afflicted for seven decades?"[68]

The explanation Yancey gives is largely the traditional one; that we live in a "fallen" physical world in which there is great beauty and order, but also great horror and disorder: "The sun that lavishes dusk with color can also bake African soil into a dry, cracked glaze, dooming millions. The rhythmic, pounding surf can, if fomented by a storm, crash in as a twenty foot wall of death, obliterating coastal villages."[69] He concludes, "Nature is our fallen sister, not our mother. And earth, God's showplace, is a good creation that has been bent."[70] He quotes G.K. Chesterton who, as a Christian, was far from convinced that this was "the best of all possible worlds." In fact, Christianity only made sense to Chesterton because "it freely admitted that he was marooned on a mutinous planet."[71]

This all leads Yancey on to say that, contrary to most people's expectations, pain, far from driving people away from God, is actually the trigger that draws them towards him: "I can turn against God for allowing such misery. On the other hand, pain can, as it did with Chesterton, drive [a person] to God."[72] And in fact, there are many instances where someone has been "laid aside" by sickness, ad has in the time of enforced rest and reflection, found the love and sympathy of God. John Donne, the English poet, and Charles Peguy, the French poet, are two cases in point. Yancey writes of Donne, who lost his wife to the bubonic plague, then fell ill himself, believing that he had also contracted the disease; and in the face of death, wrote a series of devotions on suffering "which rank among the most poignant meditations ever written on the subject."[73] Donne's *Devotions* takes God to task and accuses him, in the manner of Job. But it is also a book about facing our mortality and preparing for a good death. Donne actually did not die, but recovered. However, his poem, "No man is an island" (Meditation XVII) is celebrated as a fearless staring into the face of death.

A little later in *Where is God?* Yancey looks into the biblical writings on suffering, especially the Book of Job. He points out that Job's "comforters," whilst dogmatic and accusing, nevertheless start off on the right foot—sitting silently with Job in order to show solidarity and sympathy for him in his suffering. The test for Job is to prove Satan wrong. He does not love God

68. Ibid., 68.
69. Ibid., 67.
70. Ibid., 67–68.
71. Ibid., 77.
72. Ibid., 78.
73. Ibid., 79.

because he has many possessions and an easy life. He loves God for who God is in himself: God is worthy of his love and faithfulness. Thus, from God's point of view, some things are even more important than the prevention of suffering; namely, the freely given love of his followers. This gift of love depends upon free choice, not upon a sense of obligation. It also confers on human beings the dignity and worth of being made "in God's image."

From this Yancey moves to an important conclusion: "We are not put on earth merely to satisfy our desires, to pursue life, liberty and happiness. We are here to be changed, to be made more like God in order to prepare ourselves for a lifetime with him."[74] Like C.S. Lewis, Yancey can see much merit in the idea that suffering can develop qualities of character, maturity and wisdom. Certain moral qualities can only be honed by suffering: qualities like courage, self-giving, a willingness to endure hardship for a higher good, nobility of soul, determination to do the right thing despite the consequences.

Yancey gives a vivid picture of the opposite scenario; a world where suffering and pain has been removed. "The consequences would be very far-reaching. For example, no one could ever injure anyone else: the murderer's knife would turn to paper or his bullets to thin air; the bank safe, robbed of millions of dollars, would miraculously become filled with another million dollars; fraud, deceit, conspiracy and treason would somehow always leave the fabric of society undamaged. Again, no one would ever be injured by accident: the mountain climber, steeple-jack or playing child falling from a height would float unharmed to the ground; the reckless driver would never meet with disaster."[75] Yet the results and repercussions of such a world would mean that "there would be no need to work, there would be no call to be concerned for others in time of need or danger," and, all in all, "nature would have to work 'special providences,' instead of running according to general laws which men must learn to respect on penalty of pain or death. The laws of nature would have to be extremely flexible: sometimes an object would be hard and solid, sometimes soft."[76]

Yancey goes on to point out that in such a world our present ethical concepts would have no meaning; hurting someone would not be "wrong"; courage and fortitude would have no significance any more than generosity, kindness, unselfishness and self-control. In such a world, pleasure-seeking and hedonism would be paramount, and the development of the moral qualities which ennoble human beings would have no point. Who would want to

---

74. Ibid., 103.
75. Ibid., 101.
76. Ibid.

live in a world which had no reliable and dependable physical laws, and no inspiration or motivation towards acting well and doing right by others?

With this powerful argument, Yancey takes C.S. Lewis's understanding of the moral law underlying all things a step or two further. He then goes on to a conclusion similar to Lewis's, that a world which contains suffering is also a world which produces heroes and hope in the face of death (and he quotes from Hebrews chapter 11 in this context). He tells several longish stories about people who have had to endure long-term suffering, particularly as quadriplegics. From such real life tales, he concludes that *our response to suffering* is of vital importance. If we never come to terms with suffering, we live with constant regret, frustration and anger with God. But we only damage ourselves, have bitterness in our hearts and make no progress in our lives. On the other hand, if we accept our fate as something we can turn to good purpose in some way, then we can regain a useful and valuable life, and also regain a measure of contentment and fulfilment. He quotes in this regard the case of Joni Eareckson Tada, who used her wheelchair-bound state to encourage other paraplegics. She has addressed countless audiences about how she not only came to terms with her condition, but even turned it to advantage.

Yancey goes on further to highlight the instances of people who have accepted great suffering to further a noble cause. He gives the examples of Martin Luther King, Mahatma Gandhi, Solzhenitsyn, Desmond Tutu and Nelson Mandela, among others. He calls their persistence in the face of persecution "creative suffering."

The last part of Yancey's first book looks at how we can help and assist those who are suffering. He draws attention to the importance of "presence" and showing love—especially to any who think that God has abandoned them. He takes to task the impersonal and cold treatment of patients in hospitals and argues that a feeling of loss of control and abandonment is very bad for patients. In hospital, people should be treated kindly, should be informed about their condition, and should be involved in their treatment. They should also be shown how they can participate and share in the work of their own healing. Pain which is imbued with meaning makes it better, or easier to bear. But what the sufferer needs most is *love*: "a suffering person needs love, and not knowledge and wisdom."[77] Yancey quotes in this regard Jean Vanier, the founder of L'Arche movement: "Wounded people who have been broken by suffering and sickness ask for only one thing: a heart that loves and commits itself to them, a heart full of hope for them."[78]

77. Ibid., 187.
78. Ibid.

Yancey finishes this tour de force by focussing on the benefits of faith and hope on the sufferer, for the mind and spirit are intimately bound up with the physical state of a person and can affect that state. He also believes that faith and hope prepare the sufferer for the final and future healing, which is eschatological. We will return to this theme shortly, but for the present let us move onto Philip Yancey's second book on suffering, *The Question That Never Goes Away*.

Yancey first gives us an insight into what sparked his interest in the subject of God and suffering: he lost his father when he was only one year old. His father contracted polio and was placed in a lung machine. Many people prayed for him, and Yancey's mother was persuaded he would be healed. The medical staff removed the iron lung, but two weeks later Mr. Yancey senior died.

Between writing his two books on this subject, Philip Yancey received over one thousand letters from people struggling with the old conundrum, "Why does a loving God allow such suffering in the world?" Yancey faces this question squarely once more in the second book, speaking to individuals and groups in the aftermath of the most terrible tragedies: natural disasters, a Sarajevo ravaged by war, the Japanese tsunami which killed 19,000 people in March, 2011; and then in Newtown, Connecticut in late 2012 after the Sandy Hook School massacre (when twenty first graders and six teachers and staff were killed by a young gunman). After this latter atrocity, Yancey's earlier book *Where is God When it Hurts?* was made available as a temporary free download. More than 100,000 people took the opportunity to download it.

In a sense the much later book came out of a series of troubling disasters and human atrocities, including the outrage of bombs planted near the finishing line of the Boston marathon; the explosion at a fertiliser plant in the town of West, Texas; and then the earthquake in Sichuan, China, killing two hundred and injuring more than eight thousand. All of these calamities took place in 2013.

As with *Where is God*, *The Question That Never Goes Away* is filled with real life stories, interviews and accounts of tragic events, some of which Yancey witnessed personally in the aftermath. The circumstantial detail adds a good deal of human interest to both of his books; but there is also an underlying apologetic about God's readiness to allow suffering to be visited on (mainly) innocent victims.

In the second book, the emphasis changes. There is a greater concentration on the importance of *lament*—especially in the biblical writings, and particularly in the Psalms and in the Prophets' haranguing of God. Anger and grief as an outpouring of cathartic emotion are regarded as valuable in their own right. Yancey reminds us that two thirds of the Psalms are Psalms of Lament. Here is one example from Psalm 64 (v. 3): "I am worn out calling for help; my throat is parched. My eyes fail, looking for God." This railing at God seems perfectly natural, as Yancey makes clear; "God seems to understand fully the grounds of our protest as well as our need to rage against the pain."[79] The prophets too are outspoken in their sense of injustice: "Why does the way of the wicked prosper?" asks Jeremiah, "Why do all the faithless live at ease?" (Jer 12:1) Right at the outset of his prophecies, Habbakuk accuses God; "How long, Lord, must I call for help, but you do not listen? Or cry out to you, 'Violence!' but you do not save . . . Why do you tolerate wrongdoing?" (1:1–2).

So Yancey allows more room for the natural human response of anger at injustice and grief at tragedy—and all this anger directed at God. He names this, "Calling God to account for allowing such a world to exist."[80] In the Book of Job, the "comforters" speak loftily about God, but Job addresses God directly and honestly some fifty eight times. Yancey sees this reaction to suffering as both helpful and cathartic—cleansing and purgative—because it recognizes God's presence with us in the midst of the suffering.

And indeed, a strong emphasis in *The Question that Never Goes Away* is on the incarnation—God coming in Christ to be "Immanuel," God with us in our pain and grief. God takes upon himself extreme suffering and death, in the person of Jesus Christ. Remarkably, Jesus even cries to God in lament, "My God, my God, why have you abandoned me?" (Mark 15:3) The fact that God is present even in the most dire and painful of situations—in extremis—shows that he will strengthen and help us, and not test us beyond our strength if we trust him (see 1 Cor 10:13). As Philip Yancey says, "We need an affirmation of God's Presence in our grief."[81] Thus, God responds to the human condition "not by waving a magic wand to make evil and suffering disappear, but by absorbing it in person."[82]

This "absorbing" of suffering, and of human sinfulness, is in fact Jesus's achievement on the cross—the act we call "the atonement"; which takes the sting out of our sin and enables us to be forgiven, and to enter into a new and loving relationship with God. Jesus accepted suffering voluntarily—and even took upon himself the world's suffering and grief. This is Philip Yancey's more recent understanding of how suffering can be transformed, changed and re-directed, in order for it somehow to have a positive outcome.

79. *The Question that never goes away*, 168.
80. Ibid., 59–70.
81. Ibid., 71.
82. Ibid., 72.

In Jesus, and through his achievement on the cross, suffering is redeemed. "From Jesus I learn that God is on the side of the sufferer. God entered the drama of human history as one of its characters, not with a display of omnipotence, but in a most intimate and vulnerable way."[83]

So Yancey's second book is less philosophical, and more theological; less concerned with answers to the question of suffering and evil; more concerned with how God can help us through the reality of suffering and evil. As he himself writes; "Avoiding philosophical theories and theological lessons, [Jesus] reached out with healing and compassion. He forgave sin, healed the afflicted, cast out evil and even overcame death."[84] In following Jesus' example ourselves, we must show love and compassion to sufferers, and must respond to our own suffering as he himself did. Jesus models for us the response to the paradox of a loving God and a world filled with all manner of evil.

The upshot of all this is that God should not be seen, as in the atheist caricature, as an uncaring, remote being, untouched by what he inflicts upon us human beings. Rather, God is willing to experience in person what we suffer. As Yancey puts it; "No other religion has this model of God identifying so deeply and compassionately with humanity. We go through suffering not alone, but with God at our side."[85] We could add to this, not only at our side, but also within us, in the person of the "strengthener" (or "comforter"), the Holy Spirit.

Yancey then adds another very important point when he tells us that we can be more like Christ when we act together, as a community, to alleviate suffering. As "The Body of Christ" we can bring solace and solidarity, comfort and compassion to people: "Growth through suffering is not automatic of course. Without community support and wise love, suffering can lead to isolation and despair."[86] With this community support and wise love, there is an alchemy at work which can change the complexion of suffering. Yancey explains this; "As a journalist, I have seen [this] alchemy at work in many places: among leprosy patients in India, imprisoned pastors in China and Myanmar, impoverished senior citizens in Chicago, hospice patients in Colorado, friends and acquaintances who battle cancer and other life-threatening conditions."[87]

All in all, *The Question that never goes away* adds one or two new dimensions to the earlier work, *Where is God?* The initial reaction or response

83. Ibid., 74.
84. Ibid., 74.
85. Ibid., 75.
86. Ibid., 88.
87. Ibid., 88–89.

to suffering—*lamentation*—is given a positive role and content in the later book. The tragedies and atrocities of recent times are given a human face, as Yancey investigates their impact on ordinary people who have been hurt or who have lost loved ones. But above all, a deeper understanding of Jesus' involvement in human life and especially in human suffering is examined in greater detail—both from a theological and from a human standpoint. The implications and meanings of the incarnation are explored; and the compassion and practical love of Jesus towards ordinary human beings is also highlighted effectively. If *Where is God?* surveys the field and seeks answers in a fairly objective way, *The Question that Never Goes Away* displays more of Yancey's human sympathy for sufferers and his deeper reflection on the way Jesus himself dealt with the problem of suffering as he encountered it in this world. The conclusion is that our response to suffering should be like Jesus' own response: show genuine love for those in trouble, work for their healing (both physical and spiritual); act in concert with others in community, and try to convince them through your faith and action that God is with them through it all.

Eschatology

Both C.S. Lewis and Philip Yancey confess that no "answer" to the problem of suffering is adequate to "explain" why a loving God allows so much evil and pain to ravage the world. It is true that a great deal of *this* world's suffering is caused by human cruelty, selfishness, greed and indifference to the plight of others. And then Christians would also argue that nature itself—the physical world—has been affected by the evil permeating the whole Earth: nature is "fallen" and does not operate smoothly and efficiently all of the time.

However, these "explanations" still leave us cold—unsatisfied and unconvinced. As the Psalmists often complained, "Why do evildoers prosper?" And the prophets would add, "Yes, and why is there so much injustice which goes unpunished?"

In the final analysis, Lewis and Yancey both see the need to widen our horizons. It is not enough to dwell on this life only. We need to be reassured that God will, in the end, overcome the twin enemies of evil and death; that he will right all wrongs, see justice done and heal the world. Christians have often been accused of placing too much emphasis on the afterlife, and on the rewards to come in the next life—on "pie in the sky" some would say. And "the kingdom of God" used to be a term synonymous with "heaven" or "the life after death." Many theologians and biblical scholars have had to demonstrate that the kingdom of God is something already inaugurated, in this world and in our present life. We are possessors of "eternal life" in the here and now; not only in the unseen future.

However, the earlier complaints about an over-emphasis on the life to come have tended to make believers—like unbelievers—concentrate and focus on *this* life exclusively. But the eschatological dimension of faith is essential and is key to understanding how God will deal with evil and sin in the longer term.

Paul the apostle was no stranger to suffering, and staked his life and faith on the promise that God would restore justice and heal the world's ills. His own life included a great deal of suffering—beatings, imprisonments, snakebite and shipwreck—but he endured everything because he had the vision and conviction of the fullness of God's coming kingdom: "for our light and momentary troubles are achieving for us an eternal glory that far outweighs them all" (2 Cor 4:17). In fact, Paul goes on, "if our faith is good for this life only, then we of all people are most to be pitied" (1 Cor 15:19).

Jesus did not only show us how to live in this life—how to serve God, how to treat one another—but he also pointed to the time when God would restore the original order and harmony that was his plan for the Universe and for human life. His death and resurrection was to mark the time when sin and death would be defeated by life. In John's gospel, Jesus declares, "In this world you will have trouble, but take heart, I have overcome the world" (John 16:33). The final book of the Bible—Revelation—speaks of a new Jerusalem and a new Earth where God will "wipe every tear from their eyes. There will be no more death or mourning or crying or pain, for the old order of things has passed away . . . Behold, I am making all things new" (Rev 21:4).

Philip Yancey uses a couple of memorable phrases to highlight this eschatological dimension to life; "I learn to judge the present by the future." The other sentence he has is this; "We live out our days on Easter Saturday."[88] In other words, people of faith live in the time between heartache, suffering and death, and the Day of Resurrection. Christians are by no means exempt from the tragedies of life, just as Jesus himself was not exempt. But the worst of all possible scenarios—the torture and execution of the Son of God—was somehow turned into victory over evil and death through the resurrection of Jesus Christ.

Yancey contends that this life is a brief moment, a sputtering flame, in the light of eternity; and therefore we need to bear in mind that, as Paul says, our troubles are "momentary" and "brief" in the context of eternity.

88. Yancey, *Where is God When it Hurts?* 249–50.

And not only that, but the Holy Spirit is given to us to help us through our troubles and to give us an assurance of a greater life to come. "The Spirit bears witness with our spirit that we are children of God" (Rom 8:16). Jesus had to go back to the Father, leaving his disciples bereft. But if he did not do this, the Spirit could not be given: "Unless I go away, the Counselor will not come to you" (John 16:7). So the Holy Spirit is the personal seal of God's presence, and also is the deposit, the foretaste of eternal life to come; a guarantee that greater things lie in store for us.

It is important for Christians in our day and age to overcome embarrassment in talking about belief in a greater life to come. It is not a form of escapism or a whistling in the dark. It is an essential part of the good news of Christ's resurrection. Most people in the modern age cope with death by avoiding it and never mentioning it. That, however, is no preparation for the coming and inevitable reality. No one can avoid death, and it is best to face it and prepare ourselves for it. Throughout Christian history, a "good death" is something to make provision for.

The Bible looks to the life to come—the fullness of God's kingdom—as something integral to faith in God. It is looked forward to with joy and anticipation. We live on a planet which, in Paul's words is living with frustration and constraint—"groaning in the pains of labor" (Rom 8:21–22). But the creation itself is nevertheless waiting "with eager longing for the revealing of the children of God" (Rom 8:19). It lives "in hope" that it will be "set free from its bondage to decay" (8:21).

Philip Yancey expresses this hope very lucidly when he says, "Christian faith does not offer us a peaceful way to come to terms with death. No, it offers instead a way to overcome death. Christ stands for life, and his resurrection should give convincing proof that God is not satisfied with any 'cycle of life' that ends in death. He will go to any extent—he did go to any extent—to break that cycle."[89]

To those who are imprisoned in suffering, paralysed in ailing bodies, we can say, "Your spirit is still free and if you feed it with hope and faith, then it will be able to look forward to the time when it *can* break free from the constraints of the present time." Many people are not healed in body or mind, despite many prayers, but those who accept their condition and make the best of it, can still look forward to the time when they will be given what Paul calls "a spiritual body"—a perfected body, through which they will be able to express themselves fully—leaping and dancing and praising God.

---

89. Yancey, *Where is God When it Hurts?*, 269.

And so Philip Yancey poses the question, "Are you missing the perspective of the universe and timelessness? Would we complain about life on earth if God permitted a mere hour of suffering in an entire seventy-year lifetime of comfort? Now, our lifetime does include suffering, but that lifetime represents a mere hour of eternity."[90] To have a true perspective on pain and suffering one must wait to understand and review the whole story. "The troubles will soon be over, but the joys to come will last forever" (2 Cor 4:18). Yancey ends his first book on suffering with the analogy of childbirth. After a comfortable time in the womb where all the needs of the foetus are catered for, the new baby then has to go through a time of discomfort, constriction, twisting and straining, pressure and pain, then entry into a dark tunnel—more pain, noise, blinding light, fear, cold and finally, hey presto, birth into a new world.

⸻

Perhaps death is like that, says Yancey. Perhaps the brief time of knowing darkness, pain and fear suddenly gives way to the light of a new life . . . "Let the symphony scratch out its last mournful note of discord before it bursts into song."[91]

⸻

Thus, we come to eschatology in the end. The hope of life to come casts a ray of sunshine on this life, because it is part of a greater reality the Christian lives in. This material world is good and life well worth living, but it is decaying; our bodies are ageing and we will die and leave this world. However, despite the awful suffering of grief, the Christian has a hope which colors death and in the final analysis, permeates death with new life and the greater hope of finding all we valued in this life, all we thought and did in this life, all the love we gave out, in the life to come.

⸻

Even in the Old Testament we find traces of this hope. Psalm 22 begins in a place of awful suffering, with the words Jesus quoted on the cross, "My God, my God, why have you abandoned me?" And the Psalm goes on to describe in graphic detail agonies which could be compared to those of the pangs of death. Yet, towards the end of the Psalm, the tone changes and the outlook becomes positive, with a glimpse of life beyond the grave: "To [the Lord] indeed, shall all who sleep in the earth bow down. Before him shall bow all those who go down to the dust. And I shall live for him. Posterity will

90. As above, 274.
91. As above, 277.

serve him. Future generations will be told about the Lord and proclaim his deliverance to a people as yet unborn" (Ps 22:30–31).

And in the New Testament, the Apostle Paul says in 1 Corinthians 15: "Thus it is with the resurrection of the dead. What is sown is perishable, what is raised is imperishable. It is sown in dishonor, it is raised in glory. It is sown in weakness, it is raised in power. It is sown a physical body, it is raised a spiritual body" (vv. 42–44). And the end of this passage states that "this perishable body must put on imperishability, and this mortal body must put on immortality" (v. 53). For the word "imperishability"—not a very inspiring or well-known word—we could substitute a short phrase, so that Paul's words would then translate more encouragingly: "This ailing body must put on permanent health and wholeness and this short-lived body must put on eternal life." We must surely all look forward to that—the time when suffering and sickness come to an end.

CHAPTER 8

INTERVIEWS WITH PEOPLE WHO HAVE KNOWN SUFFERING

The Hospice movement in Britain is of fairly recent origin, having its beginnings in 1967, when Dame Cicely Saunders founded St. Christopher's Hospice in London. The idea of a hospice was not a new one, but Dame Cicely presented a modern understanding of how care of the very sick and terminally ill should be carried out. She introduced the concept of "total pain"; meaning that sickness had physical consequences, but also brought emotional and psychological suffering. The treatment should thus be *holistic*, with palliative care, but also with a system responsive to patients' wishes and wider needs, and to the impact of the illness on the family as a whole.

There are now over 200 hospices in the UK, and the hospice movement is active in some 136 countries worldwide.

I visited a typical example; the Lindsey Lodge Hospice in Scunthorpe, Lincolnshire. I witnessed how this new approach to care of the sick had been operating there. The hospice had Daycare Patients—normally about fourteen per day with around seventy on the books. These came in for treatment and rest, but also for social contact and fellowship. The atmosphere was very different from that of a hospital. The hospice was peaceful and calm, with no evidence of haste or bustle, no extraneous noise or loud voices. Carers had time to talk to the Day patients, and a chaplaincy visiting system is in place. The patients are encouraged to engage in social or communal and also in individual arts or craft activities.

The hospice also has inpatients. There are facilities (including bedrooms with en suite facilities) for ten people at any given time.

Then there are outpatients, who actually come in for treatment over a short period of time, and for consultation with a doctor.

The hospice has a paid consultant, who is also a specialist in palliative care. Then there are other doctors who are linked to the hospice and who visit on a part-time basis. Also there is a team of paid nurses, and other staff who are volunteers—the receptionists, the chaplains, the tea ladies, the fundraisers etc.

The hospice needs to meet running costs of £2.4 million per annum, and whilst the National Health Service provides some of the required funds, volunteers must raise £1.7 million of the total. The hospice is thus an independent charity, but primarily regards itself as a welcoming and caring haven that focuses on the best possible quality of care for those who have life-threatening or terminal illnesses. Some patients come for their last days to die peacefully; others come as Daycare patients one day and week, and they might live for another ten or even twenty years in certain cases.

Whilst at Lindsey Lodge I was fortunate to speak to Alison, the Head of House. Alison had worked at St. Luke's Hospice in Sheffield and then at Scunthorpe, over a period of twenty four years (from 1992). Whilst at Sheffield she realized that there was a certain need of hospice care at Scunthorpe, and she got the Health Authority to look into this. If, however, a hospice was to be inaugurated at Scunthorpe, all the initial funding would have had to be raised first. Alison managed to organize this and to motivate people to undertake the massive task of raising all the money. The situation now is that a branch of the National Health Service grants half a million pounds per annum, but volunteers still need to raise 2.4 million towards total running costs.

I asked Alison how a hospice differed from a hospital. She told me that a hospital aimed to "cure" its patients (mainly through surgery or drugs), whereas the primary ethos of a hospice is *to care*, rather than to cure. This means the best possible care—physical, emotional and spiritual—a holistic approach to the person's well-being, and the assurance of the best possible quality of life. Symptoms of the illness must be "managed" and palliative care provided if necessary. In order to deliver the high ideals of the hospice, Alison has the help of a strong support network of psychologists, doctors, chaplains and nurses.

I asked how hospice patients react to their severe diagnoses. She told me that some never come to terms with their condition; others find acceptance, even peace of mind. She then added, solemnly, "the human spirit can cope with overwhelming situations." I then asked whether people with a faith in God found it easier or harder to cope with terminal illness. She first burst out with, "Well, I am not a believer myself." Then she added, "Some people with strong belief find it hard to cope with sickness. Others might find it a comfort." I didn't have time to pursue Alison's own beliefs or lack or faith, but I told her that I would like to be able to talk further about it another time. She smiled and seemed to quite like the idea. Alison is a remarkable and very determined woman who is full of one sort of faith— faith in the need to care for her fellow human beings, even when they are *in extremis*. She has lived a very active and fruitful life doing much good without making a big noise about it. She seemed to have found some fulfilment, despite the worry and difficulty of raising enough money to continue the great work.

In the Daycare unit of the hospice my first conversation was with Tina, who, prior to 2008, was very sporty and fit. Then, in the course of that year, she began to lose her balance, felt her legs to be heavy and was then diagnosed with a rare form of motor-neurone disease. Motor-neurone disease is very difficult to cope with, since it gradually causes the deterioration and loss of function of the motor system—mainly the nerves in the brain and spinal column which give us control of our muscles.

Tina's condition has progressed slowly and she is now confined to a wheelchair, and has lost much of her muscular strength and movement. Tina told me that receiving the diagnosis was "like opening Pandora's box." Even so, she said she was relieved to know exactly what was wrong with her. She thought things through, decided that she had done nothing to bring on her illness, so she determined not to feel guilty or bitter, but to enjoy the life she could live and had left. She swam until Christmas, 2014, but since then has had to slow down, whereas before, she had been "travelling in the fast lane!"

Tina's appreciation of nature and of the life she had grew. She loves flowers and trees, smells and colors more intensely now. She has drawn closer to her family too: she has four brothers and recently there has been more open affection shown. She had a holiday in Llandudno, where each of her brothers took a turn at pushing her in the wheelchair!

She told me she has a Christian faith, but has never been a regular churchgoer. However, the illness did not make her angry with God; it drew her closer to God. She feels grateful for the life she has had and thinks she has been fortunate to have lived life to the full until recently. Tina has found the friendship and care of the hospice very comforting, and has made many new friends.

Tina is clearly a positive and optimistic person. Her focus is largely on this life, and she is trying to make the most of each new day, and has come to terms with the limiting of her activities; enjoying what she can now manage.

Rather than displaying a deep faith, she has a natural trust and what I call an *'anima naturaliter christiana'*—a natural Christian spirit.

☙

Alan at the hospice had a seizure in January 2014, and thought it was a stroke, since it affected his movements and speech. However, it turned out to be a "golf-ball sized tumor" next to the brain. Alan is a matter-of-fact type of man, unused or unwilling to show much emotion. He faced up to his situation simply by thinking like this: "I've been at the front of the queue for being talented and a musician and for being good-looking" (modesty is not his chief virtue, apparently, although he said this tongue-in-cheek), "but I was at the back of the queue for being rich and for staying healthy." Now things have changed drastically for Alan; his diagnosis was terminal—he would probably have only three to nine months left to live. But that was nearly three years ago, and apart from some occasional speech and memory problems, Alan is still going quite strong.

He told me in detail about his brain operation, effected while he was "wide awake!" Then he endured a "horrendous" course of chemotherapy treatment, but since then for the last six months, has had no further treatment and is receiving palliative care only.

He comes in one day a week to the hospice and this helps him "to deal with psychological aspects of the illness." He bluntly told me he had been handed a death sentence. Alan knows all about this; he was a prison warden and governor for thirty years.

He told me that with cancer you are alone; hence he much values the chance to have human support and friendship. His family situation is complicated—divorced with two children and three grandchildren. His attitude to his new situation of incapacity and terminal illness comes from an adage that his father drummed into him: "Only worry about the things you can do something about."

Alan told me that he has often been in churches, because he played in a brass band for many years. "I know all the hymns," he said. He has a "healthy respect" for God, but finds religious belief "a nebulous concept." His time in church he described as "a top up." It was hard to get Alan to elaborate on this, or to talk about his personal feelings or his relationship with God, but the chaplain told me that his illness has made him think about things and dwell more on his faith, which the chaplain thought had grown somewhat. It was interesting to me that a man who is so matter-of-fact has not blamed God for his condition, but has decided to be on the same side as God! In Alan's case, however, it is not so much a matter of God working within through the Spirit, but a matter of tipping the cap and acknowledging a higher power beyond ourselves.

※

Christine in the hospice was different again. She was diagnosed with lung cancer almost two years before my visit. The large tumor had spread since, and yet she had never been a smoker. So it is no surprise that at first she felt angry and asked, "Why me?" She couldn't believe her bad luck. Even now she is having difficulty coming to terms with her situation. She told me, "I feel crap most of the time," and this is especially true after chemotherapy. Before her illness she loved to keep fit by trampolining, jogging, and skipping. Now she can still walk a bit, but that is all.

"The illness has taken over my life."

Christine has drawn closer to her children through her suffering. She has a boy and two girls. Her elder daughter is an ambulance driver who tries to keep her positive. The younger daughter does her housework and takes her out. The son visits only occasionally: I had the impression that he is finding it hard to come to terms with her illness. Christine told me that she had only had the course of chemotherapy for her children's sake. Yet she has a zest for life and still hopes to do a parachute jump! She also said ruefully, "I want to stay here."

Christine had no Christian faith, but strangely, said she believed there was something in mediums and spiritualism. I asked if that meant she believed in a life after death. She hesitantly said "yes." Then she came out with an off-the-wall comment: "I think cats are reincarnated spirits!" Christine's attitude to God is rather negative: "He doesn't help you. You have to do it all for yourself." It struck me that some more discussion and teaching about faith might well help her to see things a little differently.

Coming to the hospice was, for Christine, a very positive experience. "Amazing people, who can't do enough for you," was her comment on the staff. Although "they don't get anything out of it themselves, they are willing to put themselves out in all sorts of ways." Meeting people and making friends "takes you out of yourself." Christine did not want to wallow in self-pity.

She has a great love of animals, and would have loved to open and run an animal sanctuary. "They give you unconditional love," she told me. I wondered if she found such relationships easier than the complicated ones with other human beings. Another thing she said to me seemed to confirm my intuition: "People should be more caring towards each other," and then, "Don't take advantage of other people" was her motto. Were there hurts in her past life, I wondered?

Christine is a feisty character, full of life even though seriously ill; confused in her reflections, but with a good heart. I hope she has time to discover more of God's mercy.

⁓

Margery (not her real name) in the hospice was afflicted, like Christine, with terminal lung cancer, but she had been a long-term smoker. Her treatment had given her brittle bones, and she had in fact fractured a bone in her back, which was giving her a lot of discomfort. Her illness was diagnosed in August of 2015 and she was not given long to live. However, the chemotherapy succeeded in shrinking the melanoma. Her first course of treatment was "terrible" and took away her sense of taste. Margery knew that her years of smoking had triggered the cancer. Her daughters had taken the news badly, but her husband was very supportive. Together they had had "a lovely Christmas" (2015) and Margery insisted that it would have been better if she had gone soon afterwards. Now she is in constant pain, and her treatment is mainly pain relief. She feels guilty that at home she can't do much and has to watch others do all the chores and hard work.

Margery told me that the good result of all this was that her family had drawn much closer. She has three children, and one of them was very distant until recently. She herself values both her family and other people much more highly than she used to.

When she was having treatment in hospital she was placed in a ward with three people who were close to death. "That freaked me out!" she confessed. But since then she has been coming to the hospice and has found it easier to come to terms with her fate, and she has now refused any further chemotherapy.

Margery told me that she had gone to church when she was younger. I asked her whether she still believed in God and she said forthrightly, "If you don't believe in God, what is there?" She is not a practicing Christian, but has a strong assurance. Now she is hoping that her daughters will be able to "accept the inevitable" and allow her to die a peaceful death. This was poignant and sad to hear, but I felt that she is a woman with a great deal of courage.

⁓

Frances was another lady gradually drawing close to death, and was now an in-patient in the bedded unit of the hospice. She was diagnosed with multiple sclerosis (M.S.) twenty years ago. This would strike her every three to four months and then go into remission. However, each time that there was a relapse, she could never get quite back to the previous point.

Nevertheless, Frances was calm and serene. She was very gracious and appreciative of all the care she received from the nurses—"lovely people," she said. While I was talking to her, her daughter Jo (a hospital nurse) was in attendance. She interjected and told me that she had seen people in hospital with no visitors, no one to care. And she added, "It breaks my heart."

When she was first diagnosed, Frances cried, but since then she has become accepting of her condition, and is pleased that in our times she can have access to a motorized wheelchair and much other assistance. She told me that her experience has drawn her closer to God, and that she speaks to God every day. She added that she was "more spiritual" now than before. I felt that she meant she had more inner peace and a greater sense of God's presence.

Frances was also grateful for friends and helpers. One of her closest friends now is a pastor's wife. Some other friends she had lost because they found her condition embarrassing. She loved her home and garden . . . Frances lived in thanksgiving to God for all the little blessings of her life; and conversing with her was a blessing to me as well.

⁂

One aspect of the Hospice movement that is very impressive is the provision for family support and bereavement counselling and care. I was able to speak to Angie, the Family Support manager, who explained to me the importance of caring for patients' families, who are often bewildered or even devastated by the diagnosis and new situation. It could be a husband or wife who is having to face the prospect of life alone, or feeling guilty about what they might have done to prevent the trouble which had befallen them. They often have difficulty in coming to terms with their new circumstances.

The family support unit helps family members to think through how they will manage the future. Sometimes the members are children of a sufferer, who are themselves now senior citizens. The hospice gives the chance for family members to talk about and share their thoughts and feelings and to seek help if or when it is desired. Then after a loved one's death, family members are invited to join a bereavement group which meets for six weeks. Some take up the offer straight away, others might delay a while; some even come after a year has elapsed! This could be because the aftermath of death is a busy period of time, and the bereaved have visitors and well-wishers. Angie told me that men in particular deliberately go out to meet friends and try to avoid quiet reflection or grieving. Then at a later stage they feel the need to participate in a group. Each of the six weeks of the course takes up a different theme or topic. This includes the bringing of an item which reminds the person of their loved one, and then talking a little about it. Another week, the group is asked what they would like to say to their loved one if they were still able to. The group often forges deep bonds of friendship, thus providing an ongoing support network. If someone needs more in-depth help, they can be referred to a psychologist or a specialist bereavement organization. Some like a follow-up visit after the six weeks has ended, others simply resume life as before. There is the opportunity to come to a drop-in bereavement meeting once a month, called "Reflections."

This group offers the chance to share grief and other feelings with other people in a similar position. This means that bereavement does not have to be endured alone and people with listening skills and understanding can help. The group can become an ongoing support more or less independent of the official organization. In the case of Lindsey Lodge, a walking group linked to bereavement has been set up. This allows the members to take the lead and to set an informal agenda which might lead to deep discussion or might simply be an enjoyable day out.

Some have attended a form of bereavement group for five years or more. Many give Angie very positive feedback about this work.

In terms of faith, some members say that their faith has helped them through a difficult period; others that their faith has been tested. Others again ask for prayers for their loved one. Whichever way someone speaks or reacts, everyone is encouraged to speak without embarrassment and without restraint. Different opinions in a bereavement group are not just tolerated but heard sympathetically. If anyone seems in particular need of spiritual counsel, they can be referred to a chaplain or minister. The main chaplain, who facilitated my visits, told me that a special thanksgiving or memorial service is organized each year, when the bereaved can remember and celebrate the life of the person they have lost. All the relatives of those who have died within the previous two years are invited. On such occasions, some one hundred families might be represented. The staff from the hospice also attend and read out the names of those who have died.

I found Angie a very sensitive and sympathetic person, who clearly has her heart in the work she does. She told me that her commitment is partly due to the fact that she herself lost her own son after caring for him through an illness which lasted eighteen years.

⁋

Away from the hospice I interviewed Eleanor, who lost her mother Pippa to cancer after almost a year in which she and Eleanor's family shared the same home. We discussed the period before and after the bereavement. Pippa became very tired towards the end of March 2015 and saw the doctor, who immediately sent her to hospital. She had ultrasound and CT scans, and it was discovered that she had liver cancer which had also spread elsewhere, and which was inoperable.

Eleanor told me this was the worst day of her life. She felt sick in the pit of her stomach. But despite the terrible shock, Pippa herself reacted calmly and acted quite normally, which was to some extent reassuring. After some time the consultant was very surprised that Pippa seemed to be keeping so well, and had had few apparent side effects. The initial diagnosis was for a rapid deterioration and only weeks to live. In fact, Pippa lived for a year; from Holy Week 2015 to Holy Week 2016. Right to the end she remained active in her church, arranging the flowers, organizing various rotas, leading the Junior Church and going to services and other events.

Nevertheless, in some ways life did change dramatically for the family. Eleanor told me that she did much of her grieving before her mother's death; even though the number of visitors and well-wishers coming to the house (and often staying) meant that quiet times of reflection and moments alone were difficult to find. The busyness of the days after diagnosis meant that Eleanor went into "hyper-organizational mode." She got her mother to write a will, close down various bank accounts, put her affairs in order and clear the house a bit! Throughout all this Pippa was matter-of-fact and stayed positive. She might have shed a few tears in the morning, but she was mostly serene and full of faith; thinking of others' needs more than her own. She talked a lot to her children—especially about the future. It made Eleanor and her brother and sister realize what they were going to lose. Their father had been taken from them some ten years before and now the future looked very uncertain. Eleanor knew her own four children would suffer—her mother had been a great support as babysitter, music teacher, inspiration and motivator. The grandchildren loved "granny Pip-Pip," who was almost a second mother to them. The youngest child was even born in the family home.

People continued to visit through the entire year that Pippa had left. Sometimes it was a joyful time out in the warmth and sunshine of the garden; sometimes it was a more sombre time, as when work colleagues came to express their thanks and appreciation. Family members responded to the crisis in different ways, and later on some were eager—too eager perhaps—to join in the planning of the funeral. Eleanor found herself "carrying other people's grief." Family members would take her aside to comment on Pippa's condition or decline. One or two would speak gloomily—one in particular was still dealing with her own grief, since her husband had recently died. None of the family really seemed to understand the needs of Eleanor or of the other children and grandchildren. So she had to give out an awful lot, consoling and reassuring others—a draining process.

Pippa knew exactly what she was going through and how it would all end. She had been a psychiatric nurse and a geriatric nurse. She had also been a hospital visitor, and had nursed her own parents towards the end of their lives. In addition, she had supported her husband through his long illness, even donating one of her own kidneys in an attempt to save him. Yet despite all this, Pippa was cheerful and peaceful. She hoped the dying would not affect her mind or cause her too much pain, but apart from that, her strong Christian faith appeared to carry her and sustain her.

All in all, that last year of Pippa's life was, in Eleanor's words, "one of the best years she could have had." She had two successful treatments, and miraculously, no side effects either time. This gave her the gift of extra time and a good quality of life. Some of the family went with Pippa to the Taize ecumenical community in France. Pippa loved it and tried out her French a lot. She enjoyed visiting places and had a love of Romanesque architecture.

From January 2016 she started to become weaker and spent more time lying down, eating very little. She still managed a largely independent life, however. Then she developed a lump, a swelling, in her neck. This was a symptom of the end approaching. At length she went into hospital and the staff there took over. Eleanor wanted her to die at home, but it was not to be. Very near the end she had a visit from Eleanor's whole family. The grandchildren perked her up, and one young grandson read a bedtime story to her! She gave them all the gift of life membership of the National Trust. Eleanor and her husband stayed all that night and in the morning Pippa passed away peacefully. It was as though she had chosen her time carefully: she had the gift of a year of full life, and the gift of a good death without too much pain, at a time when the grandchildren were off school and able to see more of her and then to attend the funeral. It was just before Easter.

Some three hundred and fifty people came to the funeral in Lincoln Cathedral. It was a magnificent and fitting setting for a life well lived—a life which touched countless other lives. In death, Pippa's witness only increased. Eleanor told me that the funeral was "like her wedding" rather than a solemn or depressing occasion. I agreed—I was one of the three hundred and fifty mourners.

Eleanor's own faith remained constant throughout Pippa's tribulations and death. She was well prepared. She said that her mother (like her Dad) had been "no burden" on anyone during her time of suffering. Eleanor also added, "Mum will be a testimony to a lot of people. A lot of people will learn a lot of things from her life." After a little more reflection, Eleanor added sagely, "The biggest thing you can give is your love and your time." Then she spoke of the love and support of the church fellowship in particular: "The quiet support of the church has been lovely. It should be part of everyone's experience of faith." In other words, to be surrounded by a loving community makes every rite of passage more meaningful, and if painful, easier to bear. This was the church at its best.

༄

I conducted an interview with an M.S. sufferer quite outside the hospice, when I saw Barbara in her own home where she still lives independently. I spoke to her about her condition, but also about her caring for a husband who was paraplegic. Barbara has lived with M.S. for many years. Her first episode was when she was fifteen years old, but she was not clearly diagnosed until 1981. By then she had trained as a nurse, and, whilst working in a Lincoln hospital she met her husband Jim.

Jim had had a serious accident whilst in the sidecar of a racing motorcycle. This was in 1983. He broke his neck when the motorcycle veered out of control, and could not move much below the neck, except that he was able to use his arms a little, and with straps on his fingers, he could operate a computer. Barbara encouraged him to do as much as he could possibly do, and through her encouragement and his patience and persistence, he eventually took on a job training people in I.T. skills. Barbara met and fell in love with Jim, and they were married in 1983. Later, through in-vitro fertilization, Jim and Barbara were able to have their own daughter in 1994—a miracle baby they both cherished and brought up together. This daughter left home in 2012 to study at Liverpool University. After a number of bouts of illness, Jim finally died, in 2013, having held down a job most of his married life and been a good father.

Barbara has a relapse-remitting form of M.S. This means she might be stable for some years, but then she has a relapse. She would recover, but never fully. Being a nurse who had seen people with her condition, Barbara always had a clear knowledge of what lay in store for her. At first she had felt devastated and bewildered, and even thought the doctors must have made a mistake, but as time went on, she gradually came to terms with her plight.

Barbara is a convinced and practicing Christian. The diagnosis made her think, "Why me?" After all, she had committed her life to helping others and doing important caring work. She sometimes felt angry. But gradually she started to wonder if God had now given her a special insight into and sympathy with those who had the same condition. She also came to a realization of just how valuable life is. She now likes to live day to day, making the most of the time she has and the most of the things she can manage. So her advice to the young is, "Make the most of every day." She has had to adapt to new situations. She can walk a little, she can drive, she can ride a motability scooter and does her own shopping. She lives as normal and independent a life as she can. She values life itself very highly, and in particular values friends and community life.

Barbara is now at the stage of thinking "Why not me?" and she tries hard not to fall into self-pity or depression. She told me, "Determination is a big thing if you have an illness or a disability." Some of her own determination and optimism she learnt from Jim, who never felt sorry for himself, but always encouraged her to be positive, as he himself was. In spite of his own relative helplessness, Jim was a great support to her. Jim himself was cared for almost uniquely by Barbara at first, but gradually other carers came in to help her. Some were better than others! Whenever Jim contracted an infection or became ill, Barbara was always worried that he might deteriorate whilst in hospital, and then be forced to stay there. The last time he went in, Barbara's fears were realized. He did have to stay, and just when he seemed to be improving, there was a sudden change. He lost the capacity to speak coherently or to recognize people, and he died soon afterwards. Barbara believes he should have been transferred to a specialist unit at an earlier stage—something she suggested—and she now has many regrets about Jim's final days.

I asked Barbara about her faith and Christian life. She told me that the church fellowship as a whole was not always as caring or helpful as it might have been, but within that certain individual Christian friends had proved to be a great blessing and support. One of these she calls "my angel." She has a high regard for the ministers of the church, especially those who cared for her in her time of bereavement.

Barbara is still active and outgoing. She is support officer for the local M.S. society. Her approach to this is "always advise rather than tell people what to do." She feels that having been through her own illness, she is well placed to understand other people's feelings and reactions. She feels that God understands too, and is sympathetic and supportive. "I talk to God all the time," she added. Her faith has strengthened through her long ordeal, and she is bright and cheerful, loving and kind in her treatment of other people. Although tears are never far away, she remains positive, purposeful and proactive in her situation. Her love for other people and for God is what keeps her going.

A good friend of mine, Richard, was diagnosed with cancer of the bladder in 2009. He had a pathological fear of cancer, but when the diagnosis was given, he did not feel any shock: "I felt no fear whatsoever." He just thought matter-of-factly, "suppose I'll have to have an operation." In fact, Richard had to have two. Then afterwards, he faced several treatments: one involved filling his bladder with BCG vaccine twelve times over! Other treatments, like chemotherapy, made Richard feel very ill. Nevertheless, he still had a preternatural sense of peace—mainly owing to his strong faith in God. Richard is a priest of the Anglican Church.

He explained to me that for some time before his diagnosis he had been coming to terms with his own mortality. Between 1987 and 1992 he had worked as a chaplain in a hospice, and had followed a course on palliative care. Some other clergymen, he told me smilingly, couldn't face going into a hospice. Richard considered that coming to terms with one's own mortality made it easier to cope with illness or the onset of decline. He put it in Pauline terms: "You have to 'die' as a Christian before you can experience eternal life."

Richard faced his own mortality a second time when, two and a half years after his cancer diagnosis, he had a motorcycle accident. It was the week before Christmas. He was riding a small, 125cc bike, and was on his way to the doctor's in a nearby village. Fortunately, for this short journey, he had put on all his protective clothing and helmet. He was slowly progressing through the village (at 20–25 mph), and the next thing he knew, he was on his back in the road. There was an articulated lorry to his right and an engineering factory to his left. A forklift truck was loading large girders and taking them from one side to the other. It emerged without stopping onto the road and Richard hit a girder at shoulder height. Several inches higher, and he would have been decapitated. He was knocked unconscious; then when he came round, he was surrounded by paramedics (who had arrived promptly). An air ambulance helicopter arrived soon after with a doctor on board. The doctor's demeanor suggested to Richard that he was likely to die. The doctor's notes confirmed this later—Richard had severed an artery and had lost a lot of blood. A hematoma (swelling of clotted blood) as large as a football protruded from his left side. He had broken ribs and a collapsed lung. Part of the neck bone was fractured (the transverse processes). Despite everything, Richard once again had a tremendous sense of peace, as though all would be well. When Richard's wife was called, she was told that he had broken his neck and that she should come at once.

Richard was full of praise for those who helped him and cared for him. Everyone "was unerringly lovely." It would have been a much harder ordeal if it hadn't been for the kindness of staff. He then added, "There is a well of goodness in a lot of people." Richard then endured twelve weeks of painkillers, which did not give him much relief, but remarkably, a week later, he was well enough to lead his Christmas services from a seated position! After twelve weeks had passed, the pain also miraculously disappeared—more or less for good . . . Right from the outset, Richard had a strong conviction that he was not going to die and that God was caring for him—"I didn't need to do anything." His reflection on this today is that "God will provide the resources when you need them; not in advance, but when you need them."

He added a short time later, "Life can be brutal and painful," and then he said, "I'm a bit squeamish and cowardly when it comes to suffering." I did not have this impression at all, and realized that Richard was full of courage, faith and inner resources.

After the accident, Richard was going every three months, then every six months, for check-ups on his cancer. Every time he was pronounced clear, and now he only goes annually.

What has Richard learnt now that he has had time to look back on his sufferings? "I've learnt that you can trust God. What would I do if it [the cancer] came back? God would still be there!" He has also increased his love of life—"In my sixties I've got more of a zest for life than I've ever had." His appreciation of the gift of life has been greatly enhanced: "Life is fuller and more satisfying." And this despite the fact that "I don't have the energy to do everything." In fact, he added, "you have to learn to live with some things as you get older."

Richard now works in a ministry training institution and is happy and content—often laughing, full of thanksgiving and optimistic about life. He and his wife are also very generous and hospitable towards others.

⸺

Ann's (not her real name) is a somewhat contrasting case. Her suffering came out of a Christian life which became oppressive and caused her to become ill. Her parents belonged to a Pentecostal church with a rather black-and-white theology and judgemental attitudes to those who fell out of line in any way. Ann described this as "long-term emotional frustration" and "being in a spiritual situation which emptied me of my own personality."

At home there was constant pressure "to be good" and to comply with parental wishes. These were often portrayed as "God's will." Ann tried to please her parents and to "do her duty": she went to prayer meetings, she gave generously, she played the organ at church. Ann told me that she did enjoy the worship, but at the same time, she felt that while it lifted the emotions, it failed to feed the mind or allow questions or doubts to be addressed. I asked her if she thought the "emotional highs" were the same as the work of the Holy Spirit. As she considered this, it was as though she'd had a revelation: "No," she replied, "the Holy Spirit should bring peace and love"—and by implication she distinguished between that spiritual effect and the emotional excitement of worship and preaching.

Ann had an inner conflict between her Christian "duty" and her desire to live in a wider world and to meet with friends outside the church. Adding to the pressure was her father, always in the background, who seemed insecure in himself ("wanting to be someone" in Ann's words) and rather squashing her individuality and personal aspirations. She "tried to live his life for him." In this phrase I detected an element of pity as well as of responsibility—in other words, concern for him was an extra burden for Ann.

It ended with Ann going to psychotherapy over a long period of time. Did that help, I asked? "Well," she said, "it put me in touch with my gut feelings." She thought these were her true feelings and therefore were the voice of God within. She started to change in her spirituality and theological thinking. Now she saw God as one who came to take the burdens from her, rather than one who was always placing burdens upon her. "The Holy Spirit scoops you up without you having to stress," was one of the phrases she used.

The psychotherapist realized at length that it was not just the pressure to conform and to have the right beliefs—the attitudes coming from the church members. It was the background of a controlling father (who was nevertheless sensitive to his own feelings). Her mother too was demanding and undemonstrative. Ann was told by the psychotherapist, "Your mother never comforted you," and she came to realize that this had led to her own inner insecurity and desire to be loved. She told me she had always felt "very alone." But her needs had led her to have unsuitable boyfriends who were confident, rather controlling and out to prove themselves.

Once Ann understood herself better she "had to reverse the process." By then she was teaching full time and was becoming physically and mentally exhausted. At length she became very poorly with M.E.—a debilitating condition leaving the sufferer permanently weak and tired. She had no life outside work—getting home to lie on the sofa or go to bed. After some time, she was persuaded to retire at the age of fifty. She knew her colleagues valued her, but she also knew that they could see her condition becoming steadily worse and making her very ill.

After retiring, Ann needed two years of almost complete rest to get on the road to recovery. She gradually built herself up and could live a semi-normal life (as she does still today); but she had (and has) to be very careful not to overdo things or to overwork.

How did all this affect her faith? She told me that her faith has become broader, more patient and less judgemental. She has much more love—especially for people who are *not* Christians. From constantly trying to please others, she has moved to looking after her own well-being and loving herself. Ann mentioned the deleterious effects of a censorious Christianity and insisted more than once, "I have stopped being judgemental." She told me that "in a trusting and fair environment everyone can flourish." I asked her if her understanding of God had changed, and we concluded that God is loving, merciful and just first and foremost; and a judge only with those who are proud and self-satisfied. After all, that was Jesus' attitude: mercy to sinners and marginalized people; judgement upon the arrogance of the Pharisees.

Ann herself is a loving person. She has no reason to feel that she is not good enough to please God or others. She has many good qualities and a kind and giving personality. I realized through our conversations that a harsh and narrow form of Christianity is not only unloving, but it lays heavy burdens upon its adherents and condemns many people to hell who do not share the life and dogma of that kind of faith. But who is anyone to decide for God which people might be destined for hell? It is like a young child usurping the role of the teacher in a classroom. And who are we to judge anyway, with all our own faults, and especially when Jesus warned us, "Do not judge, lest you be judged" (see Matt 7:1–3).

The survey I conducted among people who have known and are often still experiencing severe suffering is in no way intended to be a comprehensive, or even representative, sociological review. It is a selective sample of people who have had to face serious issues or troubles in their lives. The interviews are, I hope, varied and wide-ranging enough to yield some interesting conclusions. As I look back over this relatively small sample, I do not wish to draw definitive or general conclusions, but to note themes which recur and ideas and experiences which seem to be widely shared. The following are conclusions I felt to be sufficiently widespread and important to be worth highlighting.

First, I witnessed the resilience of the human spirit. Nearly every person I interviewed displayed great courage and a desire to rise above their suffering—to make the best of things and to value and appreciate life in its glory and beauty. There is almost nothing life can throw at people, with its "sea of troubles" that cannot be endured somehow and even overcome in many cases.

Second, virtually all of my interviewees told me that suffering had enhanced their love of life and their valuing of each new day. Even those with the most restricted lives and overwhelming problems still regard life as a wonderful gift. Many commented on "living one day at a time" and "making the most of each day." The beauties of nature were often mentioned: the flowers, the trees, the mountains and valleys, special vistas and the joys of a lovely day. Many were happy just to sit quietly in a garden and admire the view.

Thirdly, I came to see that sufferers become very grateful towards anyone willing to help them and to sympathize with their condition. Family relations often drew closer—sometimes even bringing reconciliation between those who were somewhat estranged before. Friends were also greatly valued, and some I spoke to had noticed that serious illness teaches you over time who your real and faithful friends are. Doctors, nurses and staff at the hospital or hospice were also much appreciated and praised for their willingness to listen and to put themselves out and go the extra mile.

Fourthly, very few of those I spoke to felt anger towards God. Perhaps this raw emotion was sometimes an early response. And in fact anger with God or lamentation are not out of place—the Bible shows that to be the case, especially in the Psalms and in Lamentations, where railing at God is sometimes the order of the day. But Psalms of that kind usually give way to a change of mood and often conclude with praise and thanksgiving. Those receiving a bad diagnosis or being made aware of a terminal illness might similarly begin with "Why me?" or "Why has God done this to me?" But such people usually moved on to a calmer and more tempered sense of "I have had a good life, but bad luck has struck me" or "life has now dealt me a bad hand." Most came to separate God from the vicissitudes of life, and came to understand God as one who sympathized and drew alongside to bring comfort, even if he didn't necessarily bring healing.

Fifthly, in certain cases, serious illness actually drew people closer to God. They revisited or revived a faith which was sometimes inchoate or half-formed,, and moved onto a faith which was capable of consoling or even of sustaining them through the deep waters of suffering. Those who were already committed Christians either found peace and became reconciled to their fate; or alternatively, their faith might change and become more loving and accepting of others and kinder and gentler towards themselves. The duty-bound narrow faith of "Thou shalt not" or of "Don't do as others do" could be transformed into "God's Spirit is strengthening me" or "God's blessing has freed me from guilt." To my way of thinking, the sufferers often arrived at a much healthier and more fulfilling vision of God and understanding of faith than many of those who apparently "don't need a physician."

So, all in all, suffering can reveal surprising truths. Suffering is of course not something anyone should seek or desire in itself—that is simply unnatural masochism. But paradoxically, through suffering people can deepen understanding of themselves, their appreciation of others, their love of life and of the world we live in; and also, can draw people closer to God. They come to regard God as one who loves unconditionally and who cares for us, and who can be trusted. This is in line with what the letter to the Hebrews tells us of Jesus: "We do not have a high priest who is unable to sympathize with our weaknesses, but one who in every respect has been tested as we are, yet without sin" (Heb 4:15). And the same writer also tells us that "because he himself suffered when he was tested, he is able to help all those who are being tested" (Heb 2:18).

Chapter 9

FINAL REFLECTIONS

The writings of Elie Wiesel, who died in July of 2016, and whose book *Night*, about the horrors of the holocaust, was read by millions, tells the story of the concentration camps at Auschwitz and Buchenwald, where his father died and his mother and sister were gassed and where he himself managed to survive until its liberation by the Allies in 1945. It is a story that has affected many people and filled them with a determination to remember what happened and never to allow the same mistakes to be made again. Wiesel wrote, "Memory has become a sacred duty to all people of goodwill." He has taught us all that human cruelty and lust for power, the evils of racism, bigotry and contempt for the sanctity of life—in short, all the evils of human sin—must be opposed, halted and overcome. These must be replaced by love for others—not just our own family, tribe or nation. We must show solidarity with those who suffer at the hands of the sadistic and pitiless, and nurture a community spirit which pits most people against the small minority who are filled with hatred, intent on crimes against the innocent.

Today, in the times of ISIS or Daesh, and with the violence and inhumanity of vicious ideologies, the task Elie Wiesel sets us is more urgent than ever. A sensitization of humanity to the evil of self-inflicted suffering is vital and necessary. Suffering will never be completely banished from this world or from our lives, but we can do a great deal to reduce its scope and to lessen its impact. Suffering caused by man's inhumanity to man accounts for a large percentage of this world's total suffering.

Elie Wiesel also held that whilst "wise men remember best" at the same time "it is surely human to forget . . . Only God and God alone can and must remember everything." In other words, God stores all wrongs and injustices in his memory and will judge the world and its people in the fullness of time. From a Jewish perspective, Wiesel came to understand God as the One who suffers with us. When a man asked, as he watched someone being hanged at Buchenwald, "For God's sake, where is God?" Wiesel heard a voice within him answer, "This is where—hanging here from this gallows."

If we see God as almighty, all-powerful, all-knowing, we might end up with a triumphalist theology which leads sick people to believe that God will heal and help them only if they have enough faith. It can also lead to a view of God as remote, uninterested in our lives and in our plight. He is the "*Pantokrator*" seated on a throne on high.

On the other hand, if Jesus truly is God incarnate, then as we look to him we will see "a suffering servant," "a man of sorrows," one who identified with human beings at every level of their experience; even in the depths of their extreme suffering. He can help and heal because he knows exactly what we are going through and is in it with us.

༄

Writing later, and from the perspective of a German who had fought on the Nazi side, Jurgen Moltmann came to realize that it is important to understand God in terms of Jesus Christ. After being a soldier in the Second World War and then captured and taken prisoner of war, and kept in POW camps in Belgium, Scotland and eventually, England, Moltmann went through a period of disillusionment with his own nation—its culture and the dreadful impact of Nazi ideology on millions of lives; then he felt despair at the suffering and torment left in the wake of the war—the barbarism and wickedness of the concentration camps; the wilful murder of six million Jews and of many other "defective" people like gypsies, the mentally ill etc. Moltmann claimed that his guilt and remorse were so great that he would have preferred to die with many of his comrades rather than face up to what his nation had done under Hitler.

༄

But out of his experiences of mental suffering, Moltmann became a Christian. The first theology book he read was Reinhold Niebuhr's *The Nature and Destiny of Man*. This had a great impact on him and began to guide his thinking into a new direction, which eventually led to the gradual development of his "theology of hope." At length he became Professor of Theology at the University of Gottingen, where he had received his doctorate.

Moltmann's Christian faith was born out of suffering, and it was to suffering that he first gave his attention, in the classic writings of *The Theology of Hope* (1964) and *The Crucified God* (1972). The implications of his theology for the life of the Church were then explored and expounded in his third book, *The Church in the Power of the Spirit* (1975).

Moltmann's *The Crucified God* put forward the thesis that God is not impassible or unmoved, he is unlike the God of Greek philosophy who exists in a world outside time and who knows no change or decay. On the contrary, the Christian God, according to Moltmann, is One who knows suffering. Jesus knew the pains of facing his death, being tortured, being condemned unjustly, being flogged and beaten and finally, being subjected to the agonies of crucifixion. God must—like Jesus—have entered into human suffering. He must know grief at the death of his only Son, he must—through empathy—experience the torment and anguish Jesus had to suffer. Not only that, but Moltmann argues that Jesus went to the depths of abandonment by God—"My God, my God, why have you forsaken me?" was his cry from the cross. Jesus not only enters into the finitude of humanity, but in his death on the cross he enters the situation of man's god-forsakenness. This means that the cross—or the crucifixion—is not so much considered in this book as a means of personal salvation (as has often been the case in church history), but is seen as God's expression of love for humanity and solidarity with human suffering and pain. Jesus on the cross draws alongside any and all who are tortured, tormented or going through tribulations.

This is how Moltmann sums up Jesus' achievement on the cross: "The incarnate God is present, and can be experienced, in the humanity of every man (*sic*) and in full human corporeality. No one need dissemble and appear other than he is to perceive the fellowship of the human God with him. Rather, he can lay aside all dissembling and sham and become what he truly is in this human God. Furthermore, the crucified God is near to him in the forsakenness of every man. There is no loneliness and no rejection which he has not taken to himself and assumed in the cross of Jesus. There is no need for any attempts at justification or for any self-destructive self-accusations to draw near to him. The godforsaken and rejected man can accept himself where he comes to know the crucified God who is with him and has already accepted him."[1]

Taking account of all this, God should not then be turned into "a religion," so that humanity participates in him by creating religious thoughts and ideas. God does not become a law, so that humanity participates in him through obedience to a law. God does not become an ideal, so that humanity achieves communion with him through constant striving. Rather, God humbles himself, reaches down and takes upon himself the eternal death of the godless and the godforsaken; so that all the godless and godforsaken

---

1. Moltmann, *The Crucified God*, 286.

can, if they so wish, experience communion with him. In short, God comes to us in the Holy Spirit, the witness within, and the power in the world. And he makes himself available—as Jesus did—to all people who call upon him. Thus, Moltmann's theology is radically and fundamentally Trinitarian.

Seeing Jesus as God incarnate means that God himself identifies with humans in their suffering and alienation above anything else. For a person to draw close to God, what is therefore required is *humility*, and what can be experienced in this way is the comfort and strength of the Holy Spirit within—the One who can pray on our behalf, the One who makes God real to us as our father, and the One who witnesses with our Spirit to the truth that we are children of God.

This vision of God as involved in the world and in our lives and hearts further recognizes God as *the source* of our life who teaches us how suffering can be redeemed, by turning it, through God's help, to good ends. Such good outcomes from evil troubles might include the enabling of the human spirit to rise above adversity, thus demonstrating qualities like endurance, courage and nobility of soul. Other outcomes are often particular to a person's individual suffering and might include things like the increase of love in the family circle, the discovery of new and deep friendships, the deeper appreciation of music, or of nature. God in Christ seems to specialize in bringing good out of evil, and "making *all things* work together for good for those who love God" (Rom 8:28).

A final thought emerging from this long meditation on God and suffering is that we are not called to suffer alone. Although Jesus shows that isolation and the desperate loneliness of being abandoned by others and by God is possible, nevertheless, most people can find solace and consolation by finding other loving souls to share their burdens. It is easy in today's world for people to say they are Christians, but to pay little attention to being part of a community or church, little attention to building up close bonds of fellowship. The individualism of the western world has led to attitudes such as "Keep yourself to yourself" or "Do your own thing." And in terms of faith it means that many privatize their beliefs and never share them.

This is not conducive to human flourishing, nor is it true to biblical Christianity. In the New Testament the community is more important than the individual, and belonging is more important than making one's own choices. Even Paul, often seen as a solo operator, almost always writes his letters and heads them with greetings from himself *and others*. He might be working with Sosthenes (1 Cor) or Timothy (2 Cor, Phil, and Col) or Silas and Timothy (1 and 2 Thess) or even "all the members of God's family who are with me" (Gal). Only in the "circular" letters (Rom, Eph) does Paul write on his own authority alone. And he mostly addresses "all the saints" in a particular location—that is, all the members of the various housegroups. He rarely writes to an individual, unless it is a personal appeal (Phil, Titus).

It is Paul who understands the church as "the body of Christ," with all the theological charge that such a title carries. It is the people together who represent and present Christ to the world. It is they who together have the gifts and graces that can carry out Christ's mission. It is they together who learn how to grow and mature into a harmonious team through living and working together. It is they together who complement one another and enable the whole body to function properly. Solo Christianity is not in Paul's purview. It is the community, the fellowship, the body that effects the mission of God in the world. And today it is better, if anyone has to suffer, that others support, help and comfort. Deep friendships make suffering a more bearable affliction. As Paul himself says: "When one member suffers, we all suffer together with them; if one member is honored, we all rejoice together with them" (1 Cor 12:26).

Perhaps for those who suffer, but who have many close friends and a loving family, there is not only a suffering together, but paradoxically also a rejoicing together. Suffering alleviated by laughter and love is suffering consoled and sometimes even healed. And if our sufferings are not healed in the present time, we can look forward to the future with hope, when our decaying bodies put on a new spiritual body, and our mortal bodies take on an eternal form and are fitted for a new life in a new world (see 1 Cor 15:42–57).

BIBLIOGRAPHY

Aczel, Amir D. *Why Science Does not Disprove God.* New York: HarperCollins, 2014.
Balthasar, Hans Urs von. *The Glory of the Lord.* Edinburgh, Scotland: T. & T. Clark, 2012.
Bancewicz, Ruth. *God in the Lab: How Science Enhances Faith.* Oxford: Monarch, 2015.
Bentley Hart, David. *Atheist Delusions: The Christian Revolution & Its Fashionable Enemies.* Chelsea, MI: Sheridan, 2009.
———. *The Experience of God: Being, Consciousness, Bliss.* New Haven: Yale University Press, 2013.
Berger, Peter. *Redeeming Laughter: The Comic Dimension of Human Experience.* Berlin: de Gruyter, 2014.
Bible. Old Testament quoted from New Revised Standard Version (NRSV). New Testament: my own translation from the Greek.
Blake, William. *Songs of Innocence and Songs of Experience.* Oxford: Oxford University Press, 1970.
Boyd, Gregory. *Is God to Blame? Beyond Pat Answers to the Problem of Suffering.* London: IVP, 2003.
Burrell, David. *Deconstructing Theodicy: Why Job has Nothing to Say to the Puzzle of Suffering.* Grand Rapids, MI: Brazos, 2008.
Chesterton, G. K. *Tremendous Trifles.* London: Methuen, 1909.
Collins, Francis. *The Language of God: A Scientist Presents Evidence for Belief.* London: Pocket, 2007.
Crenshaw, J. *Defending God: Biblical Responses to the Problem of Evil.* Oxford: Oxford University Press, 2005.
Dalrymple, William. *From the Holy Mountain.* London: Harper Collins, 1997.
Davies, Paul. *The Goldilocks Enigma: Why is the Universe Just Right for Life?* London: Penguin, 2006.
Dawkins, Richard. *River out of Eden: A Darwinian View of Life.* London: W & N, 2015.
———. *Unweaving the Rainbow.* London: Penguin, 2006.
Flew, Antony. *An Introduction to Western Philosophy* London: Thames & Hudson, 1989.
———. *There is a God: How the World's Most Notorious Atheist Changed his Mind.* New York: Harper Collins, 2008
Forster, Roger. *Suffering and the God of Love: The Book of Job.* London: Push, 2006.
Gill, Robin. *Why Does God Allow Suffering?* London: SPCK, 2015.
Goodenough, Ursula. *The Sacred Depths of Nature.* Oxford: Oxford University Press, 2000.

James, William. *The Varieties of Religious Experience*. London: Penguin, 1982.
Kempis, Thomas. *The Imitation of Christ*. London: Collins Fontana, 1963.
Kung, Hans. *On Being a Christian*. New York: Doubleday, 1976.
Lewis, C. S. *A Grief Observed: Reader's Edition*. London: Faber & Faber, 2015.
———. *Mere Christianity*. London & Glasgow: Collins Fontana, 1967.
———. *The Problem of Pain*. Glasgow: Collins, 1978.
Manley Hopkins, Gerard. *Selected Poems*. Oxford: Oxford University Press, 1996.
Mayne, Michael. *The Enduring Melody*. London: Darton, Longman & Todd, 2006.
———. *The Sunrise of Wonder*. London: Darton, Longman & Todd, 2008.
McCloskey, H. J. "Good and Evil." In *Philosophical Quarterly 10*, 1960.
McGrath, Alister. *The Open Secret: A New Vision for Natural Theology*. London: Wiley-Blackwell, 2008.
McLeish, Thomas. *Faith and Wisdom in Science*. Oxford: Oxford University Press, 2014
Miller-McLemore, Bonnie J., ed. *The Wiley Blackwell Companion to Practical Theology*. Oxford: J. Wiley & Sons, 2014.
Miller, R.W., ed. *Suffering and the Christian Life*. New York: Orbis, 2013.
Moltmann, Jurgen. *The Crucified God*. 4th ed. London: SCMP, 2013.
———. *The Trinity and the Kingdom*. Minneapolis: Fortress, 1993.
Niebuhr, Reinhold. *Discerning the Signs of the Times*. New York: Scribner, 1946.
Otto, Rudolf. *The Idea of the Holy*. Translated by John W. Harvey. Oxford: Oxford University Press, 1978.
Rahner, Karl. *Man at Play*. London: Burns & Oates, 1965.
Rohr, Richard. *Job and the Mystery of Suffering*. New York: Crossroad, 2006.
Schaap, Rose. *Drinking with men: A Memoir*. New York: Riverhead, 2013.
Scruton, Roger. *The Face of God*. London: Bloomsbury, 2012.
Skevington, Wood A. *The Burning Heart: John Wesley, Evangelist*. Exeter: Paternoster, 1967.
Soelle, Dorothee. *Suffering* Philadelphia: Fortress, 1975.
Strobel, Lee. *The Case for Faith*. Grand Rapids, MI: Zondervan, 2000.
Swinton, John. *Raging with Compassion: Pastoral Responses to the Problem of Evil*. Grand Rapids, MI: Eerdmans, 2007.
Talbert, C. *Learning through Suffering: The Educational Value of Suffering in the New Testament and in its milieu* Minnesota: Liturgical Press, 1991
Thompson, Michael. *Where is the God of Justice? The Old Testament and Suffering*. Eugene, OR: Pickwick, 2011.
Tolstoy, Leo. *War and Peace*. 2 vols. London: Penguin, 1964.
Wiesel, Elie. *Night*. London: Penguin, 2008.
Worth, Jennifer. *Call the Midwife*. London: Phoenix, 2002.
Yancey, Philip. *The Question That Never Goes Away: What is God up to in a World of Such Tragedy and Pain*. London: Hodder & Stoughton, 2013.
———. *Where is God When it Hurts?* Grand Rapids, MI: Zondervan, 1977.
Yancey, Philip, and Paul Brand. *Fearfully and Wonderfully Made*. Grand Rapids, MI: Zondervan, 1980.

www.ingramcontent.com/pod-product-compliance
Lightning Source LLC
Chambersburg PA
CBHW050815160426
43192CB00010B/1771